NEW 3D EFFECTS IN GRAPHIC DESIGN

2D Solutions for Achieving
the Best Pop-Up Results

NEW 3D EF-
FECTS IN GRAP
-HIC DESIGN

FLAMANT 11

Edited by Design 360° Magazine

NEW 3D EFFECTS IN GRAPHIC DESIGN

2D Solutions for Achieving the Best Pop-Up Results

Copyright © 2019 by Sandu Publishing Co., Ltd.
Copyright © 2019 English language edition by
Flamant for sale in Europe and America.
Flamant is a brand of:
Hoaki Books, S.L.
C/ Ausiàs March 128.
08013 Barcelona, Spain
Phone: 0034 93 595 22 83
Fax: 0034 93 265 48 83
info@hoakibooks.com

Sponsored by Design 360°
– Concept and Design Magazine
Edited and produced by
Sandu Publishing Co., Ltd.
Book design, concepts & art direction by
Sandu Publishing Co., Ltd.
info@sandupublishing.com

Publisher: Sandu Publishing Co., Ltd.
Executive Editor: Anton Tan
English preface revised by: Tom Corkett
Design Director: Wang Shaoqiang
Designer: Liu Xian
Sales Managers: Niu Guanghui (China),
Winnie Feng (International)

Cover Design: Liu Xian
Front cover concept by Diego Pinilla Amaya
Back cover concept by Tina Touli

ISBN: 978-84-17084-10-3
D.L.: B 28702-2018

Printed in China

— CONTENTS —

PREFACE

It is amazing how the world that we live in provides us with so much inspiration for creativity. Our world is dominated by three-dimensional space. But for most people, graphic design is usually seen as a two-dimensional space, even if it belongs in this three-dimensional world that we live in.

In this contemporary era, we are overloaded with information and messages conveyed through a great variety of visual formats. Are we drowning in a sea of messages and ideas that get lost? Is communication becoming less effective? And can the possibilities offered by implementing the third dimension in the two-dimensional graphic design world solve these problems?

If we think about graphic design, two-dimensional graphics are the first thing that comes to our minds. The third dimension has always been a part of graphics, even if it is only present in the designer's unconscious mind when he or she is creating. Nevertheless, the third dimension used to be less important within graphic design than it is now. Three-dimensional elements are becoming more and more regular in design projects.

A great idea is not always enough. Its execution is really important. How can we achieve the best possible impact and an innovative design solution?

It all starts from a brief or perhaps from an idea in the case of a self-initiated project. As designers, we try to think differently, and our main goals are audience engagement and clear communication. We try to find unique ways to approach each project in order to prevent stagnation and create something new.

Nowadays, a designer who relies purely on means of expression such as graphics, typography, and other design elements and who only uses a two-dimensional space when developing a project will not always manage to meet that project's needs and goals. Unique design concepts sometimes cannot be easily conveyed through two-dimensional design solutions, which can be limited when it comes to efficient problem solving and creativity. A desire to "escape" from a purely two-dimensional design can help graphics to stand out.

When designers step into the three-dimensional world, they discover a whole new space that offers unlimited prospects for innovative design solutions and experimentation. Designing in three dimensions is therefore much more than a trend, and the point is not to embrace the third dimension just because it is fashionable. Good design is timeless, simple, and effortless. The challenge is to implement the third dimension in graphic design pieces in cases where the message that needs to be communicated cries out for this treatment. It is an impactful tool that not only invites the viewer to read the messages that it conveys but also takes him or her on a journey through a world that exists in parallel to our own. It brings graphics to life and allows them to stand out and work efficiently.

Ideas can be empowered by communicating with people in an honest and familiar way. In this new digital era, human nature and clear communication can be restored through a "tactile" approach to design. Even if three-dimensional graphics are presented to the viewer in a two-dimensional context that lacks a tactile materiality, they still give the viewer a sense of tactility. And they also allow us to bring the three-dimensional element of the world that we live in to our designs. Strong and memorable experiences can be created through a simple message in combination with the viewer's visual and "sensory" involvement in the design.

You are probably reading these words from a page of the print version of this book, a space that could be described as two dimensional when the page is lying flat. Yet a book is a three-dimensional object. By flipping through the pages of this book, you will start a journey into a three-dimensional world through its graphics. The worlds we see on these pages are the new worlds that we are invited to explore. Those worlds live in their creators' minds. But the most exciting part is that all of these three-dimensional worlds can appear on just printed pages—two-dimensional surfaces. Our eyes do not necessarily need an actual three-dimensional design to experience a sense of space. It is amazing how our imagination is able to transform two-dimensional graphics into the three-dimensional world represented.

What is graphic design? What can it be when it occupies a three-dimensional space? In this book, designers from all over the world who have taken this approach to invite us to celebrate unique ideas and challenge us to see the possibilities of this "new" world. The third dimension in graphic design, along with our imagination, has the power to be our strongest asset.

Tina Touli
Graphic Communication Designer
tinatouli.com

BRANDING

Design:
— **Johanna Dahmer**
— **Lena Cramer**

Client:
— **GWA**
— **Hochschule Düsseldorf**

Kosmos der Ideen

In 2018 the GWA Junior Agency Day took place in Hochschule Düsseldorf. The designers did the whole corporate design including naming and storytelling which is all about "Kosmos der Ideen (Cosmos of Ideas)." The white frame stands for the university context, in which the whole competition takes place. The planets symbolise different universities with their own ideas. The planets are moving and morphing, which show the intersection of different solutions.

Graphic Design:
— **Elvis Benicio**
— **Diego Bolgioni**

Motion Graphic:
— **Rafael Fernandes**

Client:
— **Sweet Films**

— Sweet Films

EBstudio was invited to create a new visual identity for Sweet Films that can adapt to the new strategic position and vision. Sweet Films is a Brazilian boutique studio specialised in video production for advertisements. After going through many possible ideas about shapes and graphic concept, EBstudio realised that it could be interesting to build a metaphorical connection between a fly (as a client) and something that looks yummy (sweet).

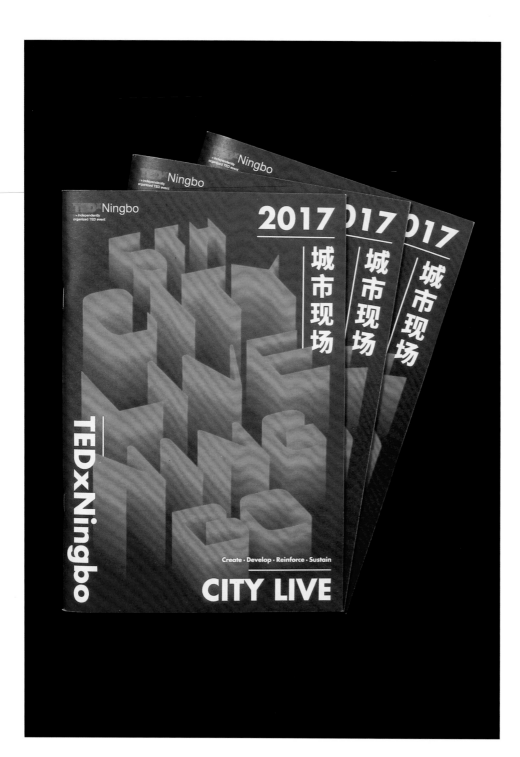

Art Direction:
— **Tseng Kuo Chan**

Design:
— **Tseng Kuo Chan**
— **I-Mei Lee**

2017 TEDx
— Ningbo City Live

The theme of 2017 TEDxNingbo is "City Live." The designers utilised the lettering and gradient technique to construct an overlooked angle. That is also the key vision of the 2017 TEDxNingbo. The blue background reflects the imagery of Ningbo as a coastal city. Meanwhile, the red colour acts in cooperation with the standard colour of TED. The gradient effect of those two colours shows that Ningbo is holding the activity of TED and represents the vivid atmosphere.

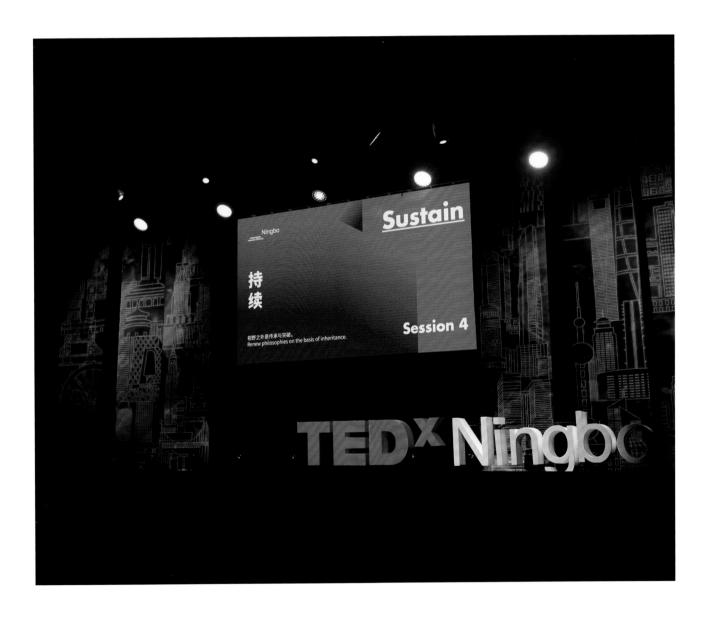

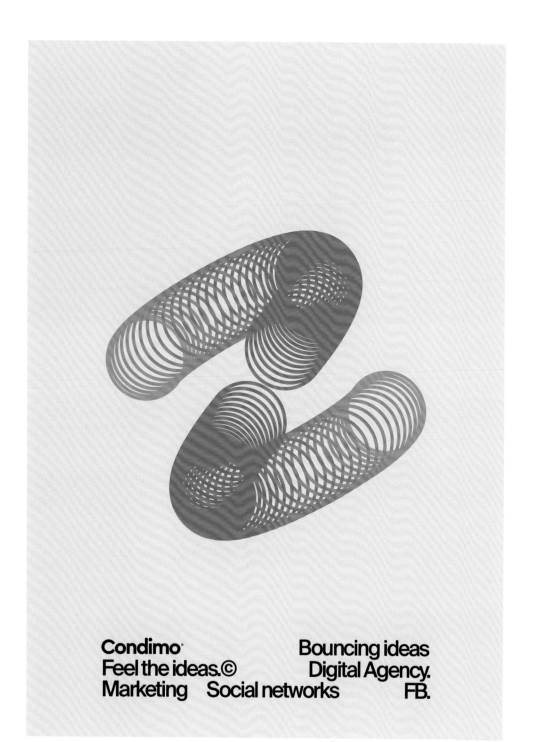

Design Agency:
— h3l™ Branding Agency

Client:
— Condimo

Condimo·
Feel the ideas.©
Marketing   Social networks

Bouncing ideas
Digital Agency.
FB.

Condimo
— **Branding Identity** —

Condimo is a concept of organic reflection, virtualisation, journey, and spontaneous interaction. The branding creation was inspired by light and the heterogeneous behaviour on its assimilation. The branding represents an open system that displays its elements in a versatile and playful way. The light colours of the palette and sans-serif fonts emphasise modernity and clean layouts in coexistence with multiple possibilities of use.

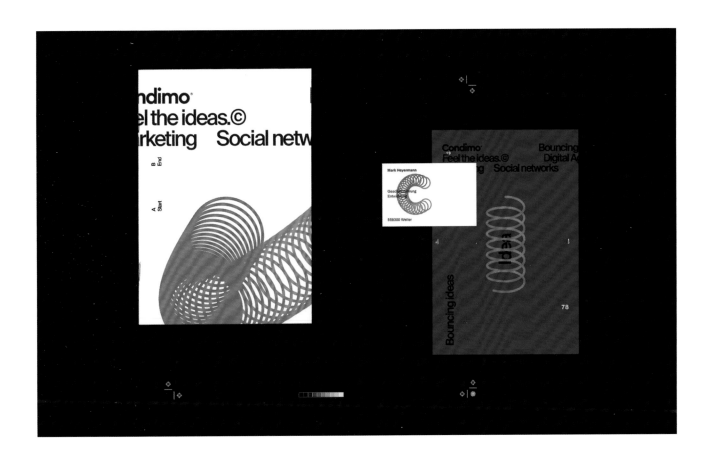

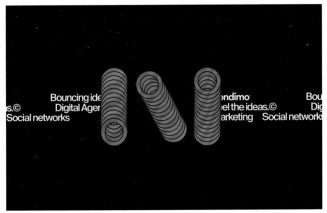

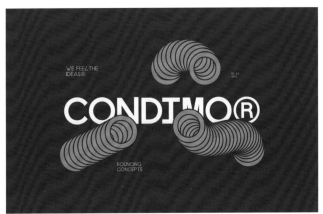

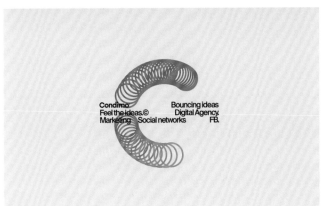

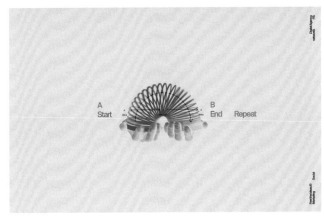

Design Agency:
— another design

2018 Shenzhen
— Design Week

As the theme of 2018 Shenzhen Design Week is "Possibilities of Design," another design invited professional designers, design enthusiasts, and the general public to complete the design together. The designed works were saved and submitted to an official app. Viewers could give "likes" to the works posted in the app. Another design then chose the works that gained more "likes" as the design elements and used them on outdoor advertisements, publicity materials, and so on.

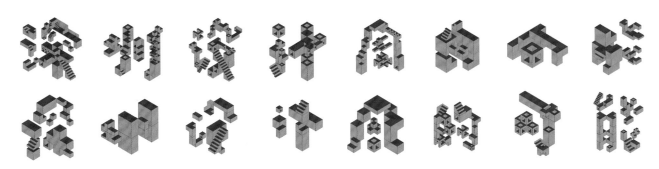

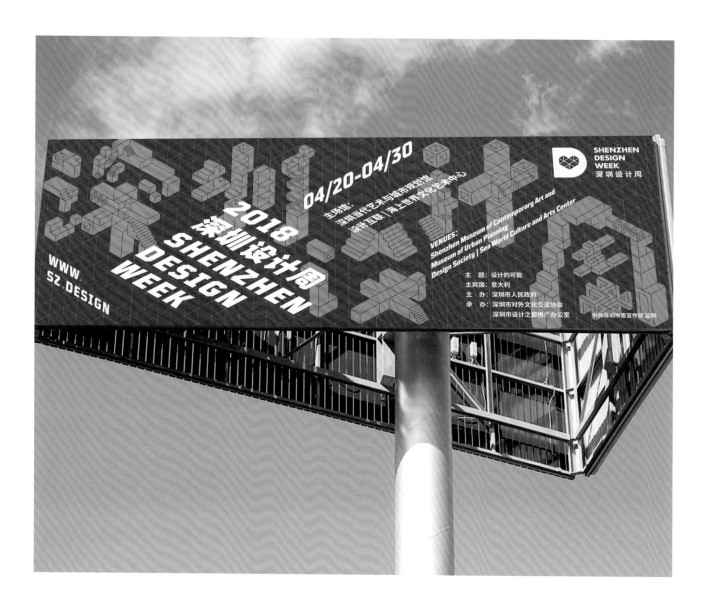

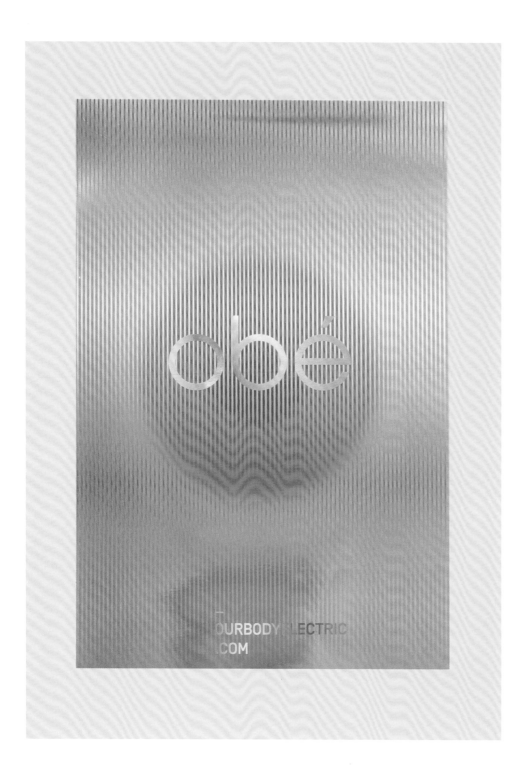

Design Agency:
— **Futura**

Client:
— **Ashley Millst**

Photography:
— **Rodrigo Chapa**

___ Obé

Obé is an app for online exercise routines and classes. The task of Futura was to give Obé's branding an upgrade. Futura created the design that communicates the power and innovation of Obé, which makes it stand out from the conventional training programmes with an avant-garde and highlighted look.

BACHELOR OF
ARTS (FINE ART)
GRADUATION
EXHIBITION
2016
藝術文學士畢業展
二零一六

24 JAN
-
15 FEB
2016

THE GALLERY WILL BE CLOSED IN
OBSERVANCE OF CHINESE NEW YEAR
FROM 8-10 FEB 2016
展覽將於二零一六年二月八至十日
農曆新年期間關閉

10:00 - 20:00

4/F - 5/F
PAO GALLERIES
HONG KONG ARTS CENTRE
2 HARBOUR ROAD
WAN CHAI, HK

香港灣仔港灣道二號
香港藝術中心
四至五樓包氏畫廊

OPENING RECEPTION
開幕典禮
23 JAN 2016
17:30 - 20:30

SPONSOR ACKNOWLEDGEMENT/
SPEECHES BY GUESTS
謝辭及嘉賓致辭
17:30 - 18:00

THE BACHELOR OF ARTS
(FINE ART) PROGRAMME
IS CO-PRESENTED BY
THE RMIT UNIVERSITY AND
THE HONG KONG ART SCHOOL

藝術文學士課程由
澳洲皇家墨爾本理工大學與
香港藝術學院合辦

RMIT
UNIVERSITY

Design Agency:
— Pengguin

Design:
— Todd Lam
— Soho So

Client:
— Hong Kong Art School

HEADLINING SPONSOR   MAJOR SPONSORS   CONTRIBUTING SPONSORS   BEVERAGE SPONSOR   PAPER SPONSOR

Burger COLLECTION®   Aesop. ASIA ONE Celebrity X Cruises® hanart TZ Gallery 漢雅軒 Nikon SPRING   ALISON PICKETT   JERSEN   Nu Skin   PaperOne

2016 BAFA
Graduation Exhibition

Capturing the spirit of the current age, the exhibition title "INCITE"—a word often used to describe rebellion or words into action—reflects the distinct energy of the graduates that have harnessed into their works over the past three years for the programme. The exhibition incorporates new perspectives, questions the status quo, and showcases the pursuit of new ways of thinking. The fire red of the geometric shapes represents the explosion of inspiration and potential from the graduates.

Design Agency:
— **Pinchof**

Art Direction:
— **Dávid Koronczi**
— **Juraj Mydla**

Graphic Design:
— **Dávid Koronczi**
— **Romvn Mikláš**

Web Developement:
— **Gábor Jénei**

Project Management:
— **Martina Szabóová**

— Nu Dance Fest 2017

Nu Dance Fest is an international venue focusing on contemporary dance and physical theatre. It was established in Bratislava, Slovakia, 2006. The ambition of Pinchof was to create a playful visual communication design for the 2017 event. In order to echo the idea "bind to movement," Pinchof created various beach balls symbolising dopamine molecules.

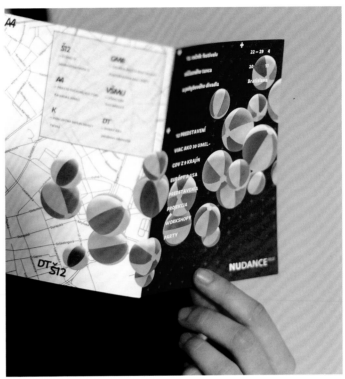

Design Agency:
— **Murmure**

Art Direction:
— **Julien Alirol**
— **Paul Ressencourt**

Creative Code:
— **Giulian Drimba**

Client:
— **Arts Attacks!
Association**

Nördik Impakt 19

Arts Attack! Association has entrusted Murmure with the global communication strategy of Nördik Impakt's 19th annual festival. Murmure has developed an experimental concept around generative design, a new territory for digital and creative expression. Murmure has set up a strong, electronic, and elegant artistic direction which enables the overall marketing campaign to be directly generated in high definition.

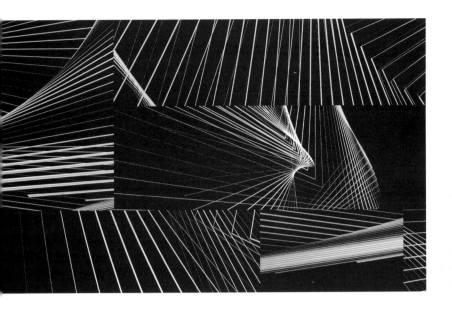

Design Agency:
— **Woka Studio**

Design:
— **David Padilla**
— **Aníbal García**

Art Direction:
— **David Padilla**
— **Aníbal García**

ING

ING is a creative festival campaign. Woka Studio's proposal for the third annual festival is based on design and technology. The main visual was inspired by the dune grooves and golden yellow colour. Those elements are generated with a pattern and adapted to forms created in 3D. Woka Studio also used a golden texture in relief. And the other visual is the overlapping circles forming the number "3."

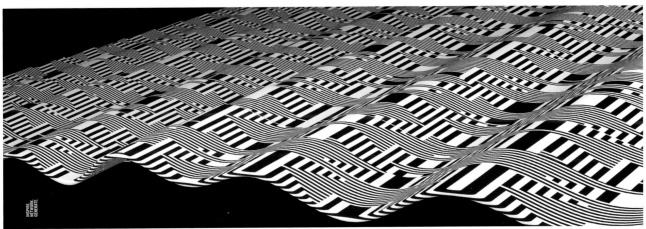

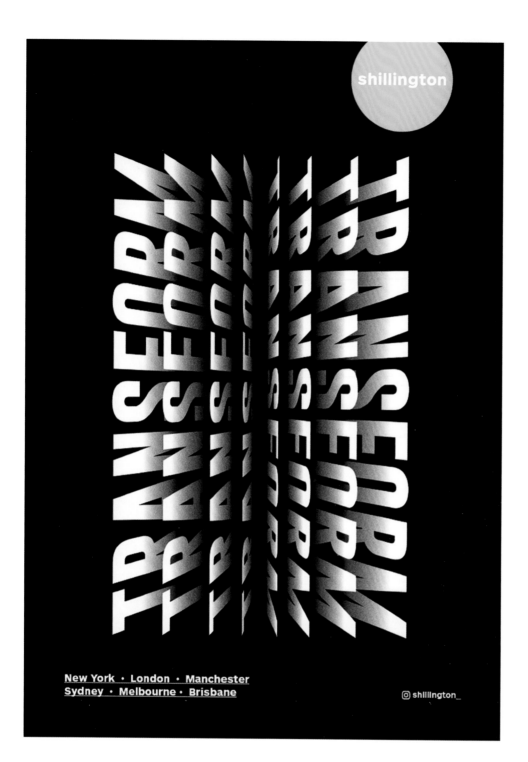

Design:
— **Shanti Sparrow**

Client:
— **Shillington**
   School of Design

Transform
— **Exhibition Identity**

The Transform Exhibition Identity was developed for the Shillington School of Design's summer graduation exhibition. The concept of transform was inspired by the student journey—from a curious observer to a passionate designer. The graphics reflect the transitional stages of change in both abstract elements and typography. This exhibition identity was rolled out internationally in New York's, London's, Sydney's, Manchester's, Brisbane's, and Melbourne's campuses.

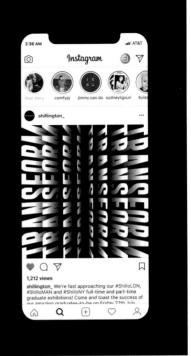

Design Agency:
— **Atelier Irradié**

Client:
— **The Peacock Society**

— The Peacock Society

Atelier Irradié was commissioned to create the visual identity of The Peacock Society Music Festival in the summer of Paris, 2017. The design took inspiration from retrofuturism and Internet art. The idea was to create a very strong aesthetic based on colour, abstract shapes, and 3D feeling. Atelier Irradié worked on a whole set of patterns that are used on different kinds of media. The iridescent colour scheme gives a digital aesthetic to the whole visual identity.

THE PEACOCK SOCIETY FESTIVAL

FESTIVAL
DES CULTURES
ÉLECTRONIQUES

WAREHOUSE VISUAL ARTS CLUB FILMS TALKS

VENDREDI **7** JUILLET 2017 SAMEDI **8**

PARC FLORAL DE PARIS | 22H > 7H

Nina Kraviz | **Dixon** | **Kaytranada** | **Marcel Dettmann**
Apollonia | **The Martinez Brothers** | **The Black Madonna**
Carl Craig PRESENTS VERSUS SYNTHESIZER ENSEMBLE | **Jackmaster** | **Moodymann** | **Dvs1**
Levon Vincent | **Midland** | **Romare** FULL LIVE BAND | **Rejjie Snow**
Tommy Genesis | **Avalon Emerson** | **Konstantin**
Jlin LIVE | Marie Davidson LIVE | Ancient Methods | Voiski LIVE | Azf
Peggy Gou | Fils De Venus | Raheem Experience (MAD REY, NEUE GRAFIK, LB AKA LABAT)
Hugo Lx | Varg LIVE | Blocaus w/ Exal | Blndr LIVE | Codex Empire LIVE
Kablam | Tgaf Crew | Bamao Yende (BOUKAN REC) | Oko Dj

INFOS & PRÉVENTES SUR THEPEACOCKSOCIETY.FR

ARTWORK: ATELIER IRRADIÉ

Design:
— Anthony Lam

Client:
— Institute of Textiles
and Clothing of the
Hong Kong Polytechnic
University (PolyU)

PolyU Fashion
— # Show 2017

PolyU Fashion Show is an annual event organised by the Institute of Textiles and Clothing, PolyU, featuring creative and talented designs of graduates. The key visual of the 2017 Show is originated from the metaphorical representation of "2017" in contrasting hues and primitive geometries, denoting graduates' uncompromising passion and aspiration to their destinies. The candy capsule impression also projects a striking and euphoric atmosphere—fashion as the remedy counteracting the chaos and disappointments in people's lives.

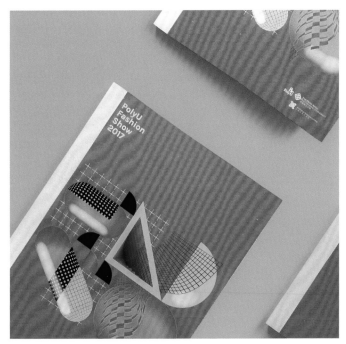
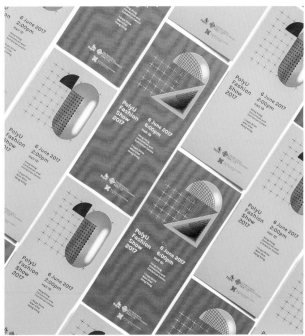

Design Agency:
— **Atelier Baudelaire**
— **GeneralPublic**
  (Jérémie Harper)

Client:
— **Mairie de Montrouge**

62nd Salon
de Montrouge

Since 2016, Atelier Baudelaire has developed a singular identity for Salon de Montrouge, a contemporary art fair next to Paris. For the 62nd edition, the design is a co-creation with Jérémie Harper from GeneralPublic. With a bold yellow neon colour that unifies the applications of the identity, the 62nd edition is characterised by glass-like 3D numbers that overlay the texts and information, making them pop out.

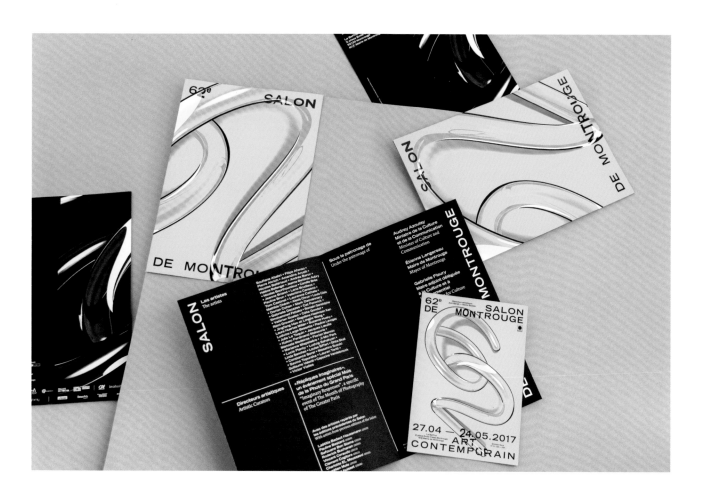

Passages Insolites 2017

Passages Insolites consists of nine playful and intriguing installations created by visual artists and architecture collectives. This project is to question people's relationship with the world and urban space. Figure was to create a real construction and then photograph them to form the visual. This construction consists of walls and lines to highlight the concepts of paths and passages, while the false perspectives, stockings, and colour combination express the unusual and creative side of this event.

Design Agency:
— **Figure**

Design, Art Direction & Illustration:
— **Jeremy Hall**

Client:
— **ExMuro**

Masterpieces Exhibition

It is the visual identity for the HKU SPACE 60th Anniversary Exhibition, *Masterpieces*. With the idea of the rising horizon, Good Morning Design created a series of promotional materials including poster, invitation, and catalogue.

Design Agency:
— **Good Morning Design**

Design:
— **Jim Wong**

Design Agency:
— **Classmate Studio**

Design:
— **Lili Köves**
— **József Gergely Kiss**

Client:
— **Brew Your Mind**

Photogprahy:
— **József Gergely Kiss**

Brew Your
—— Mind Brewery

Brew Your Mind, one of the Hungarian top craft breweries asked Classmate Studio for designing a distinctive brand and an outstanding visual identity. In order to echo their choice of brand name, Classmate Studio created the main visuals consisting of bold typography, optical illusions, and incredible 3D graphics with a contemporary colour palette.

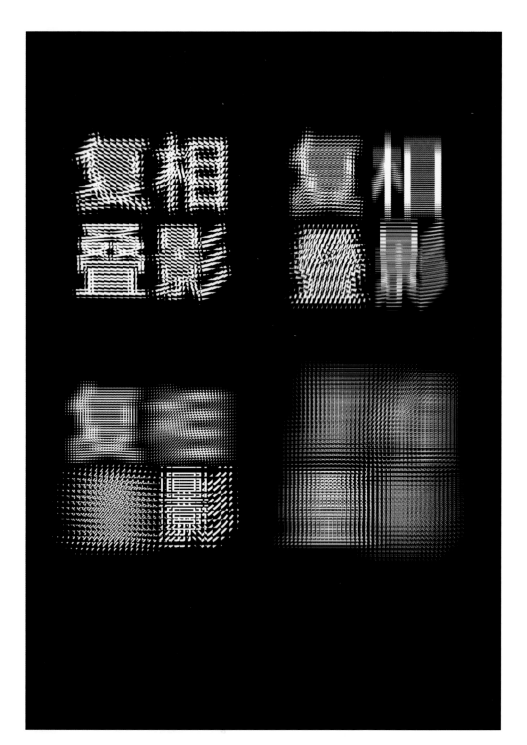

Design Agency:
— **another design**

Guangzhou
Image Triennial 2017

The exhibition theme of Guangzhou Image Triennial 2017 is "Simultaneous Eidos." Another design disassembled the Chinese characters of "Simultaneous Eidos" by computer software and made them overlap with each other, thus generated diverse styles of fonts randomly in response to the exhibition theme.

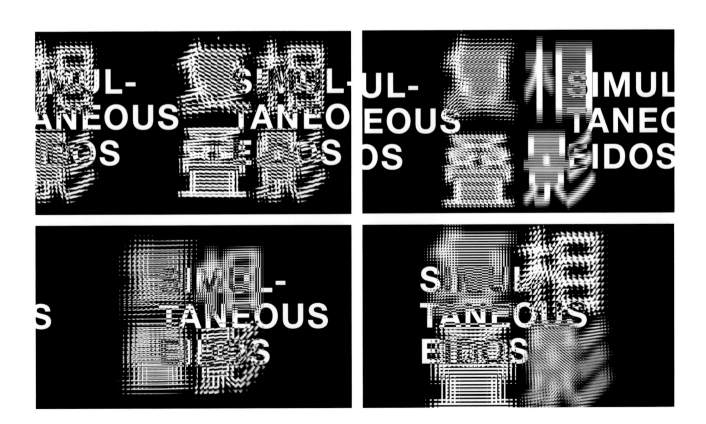

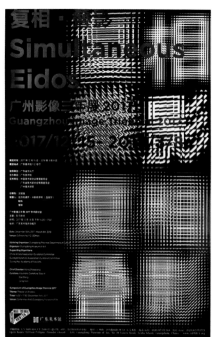

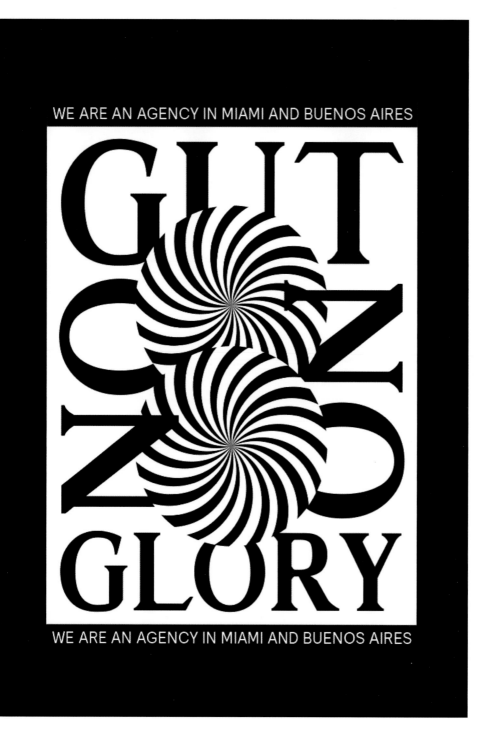

WE ARE AN AGENCY IN MIAMI AND BUENOS AIRES

GUT CON Z GLORY

WE ARE AN AGENCY IN MIAMI AND BUENOS AIRES

Design Agency:
— **Sagmeister & Walsh**

Art & Creative Direction:
— **Jessica Walsh**
— **Stefan Sagmeister**

Design:
— **Gabriela Namie**

3D & Animation:
— **Andrei Robu**

Animation:
— **Yaya Xu**

Prop Production:
— **Arielle Casale**

Photography:
— **Sarah Hopp**

Gut

Gut is an agency based in Miami and Buenos Aires. Sagmeister & Walsh created an abstract spiral logo animation inspired by guts and intestines.

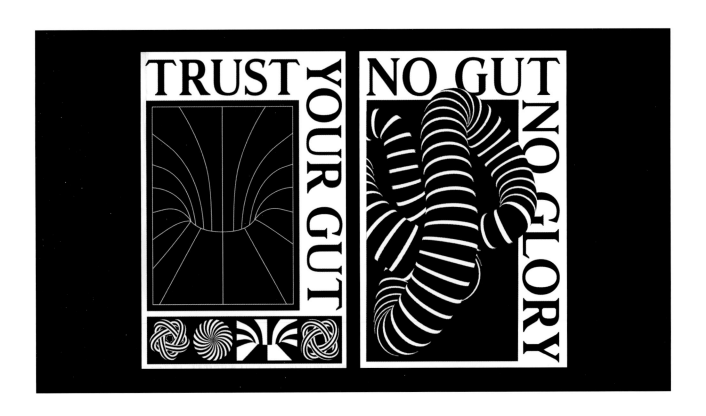

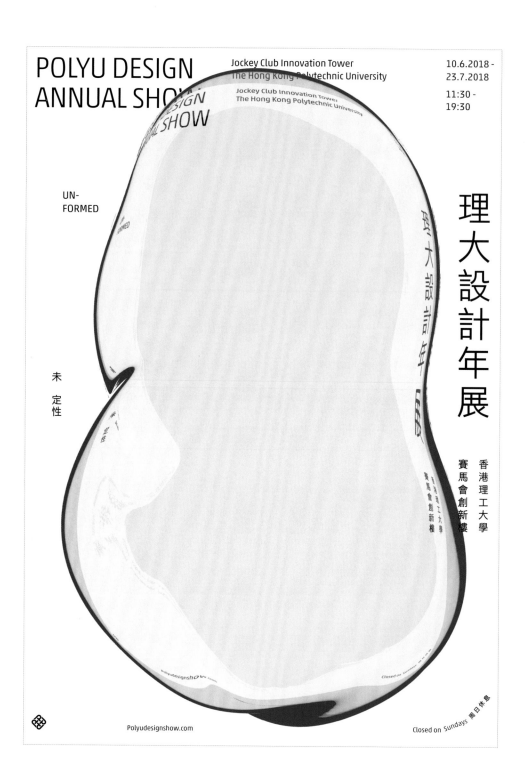

POLYU DESIGN ANNUAL SHOW

Jockey Club Innovation Tower
The Hong Kong Polytechnic University

10.6.2018 -
23.7.2018

11:30 -
19:30

Design:
— **Shui Lun Fan**

UN-FORMED

未 定 性

理大設計年展

香港理工大學
賽馬會創新樓

Polyudesignshow.com

Closed on Sundays 周日休息

___ UN-FORMED _____

UN-FORMED (PolyU Design Annual Show 2018) utilised a bubble which can keep changing its shape for visual identity in order to highlight a circumstance that there is no absolute right and wrong in the field of design. People will find the answer only if they keep experimenting and exploring. For instance, kids blow bigger bubbles when they get the soap suds. They will not be successful to blow the biggest bubble for the first time, but they will enjoy watching different shapes of the bubbles during the whole experiment.

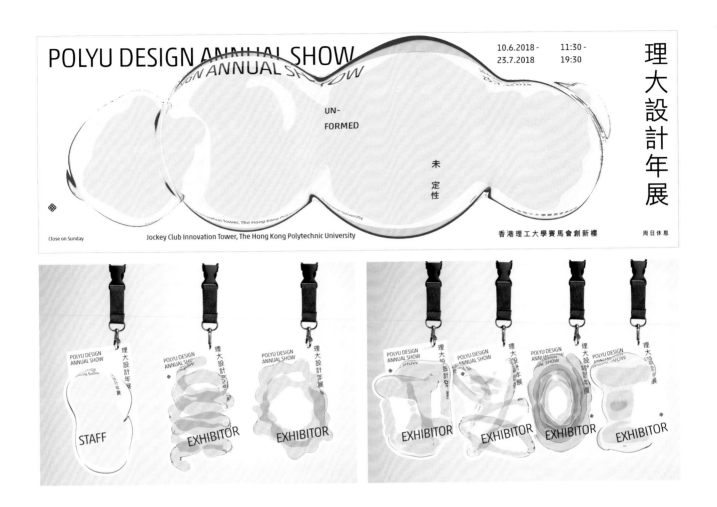

Design Agency:
— **Figure**

Design, Art Direction,
Creative Direction &
Illustration:
— **Jeremy Hall**

Client:
— **Jelimagine**

Jelimagine

Jelimagine is a company that specialises in event styling and tableware. Figure designed a typography and various materials with optical illusion so that the viewers can decode the entire message by the fruit of their imagination.

ART DE LA TABLE

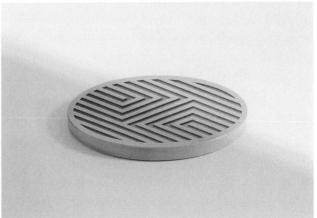

Art Direction &
Graphic Design:
— **Stepan Solodkov**

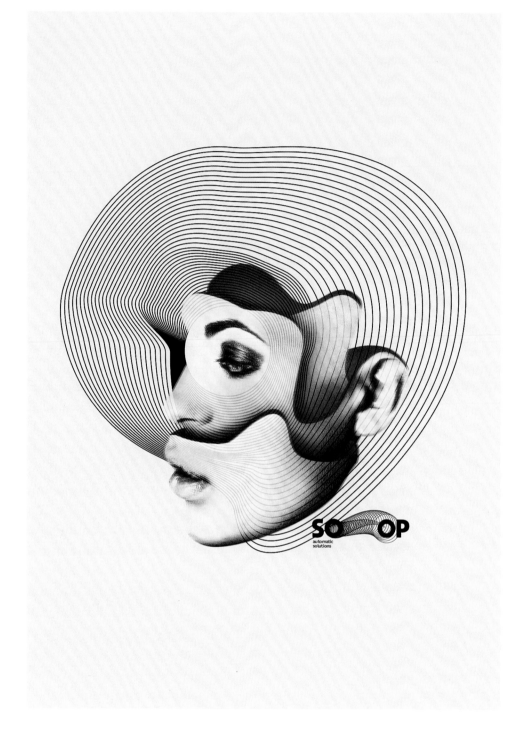

— Soop

Soop is a company specialising in the provision of services for remote administration. All the graphics in the communications are inspired by futurism and the technology of transmitting information on the waves.

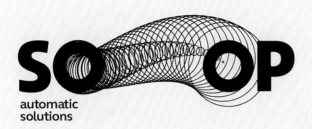

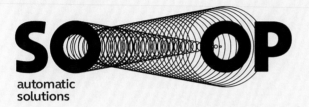
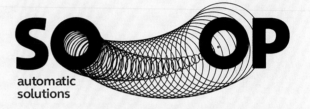
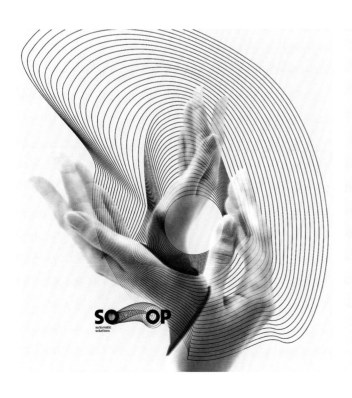

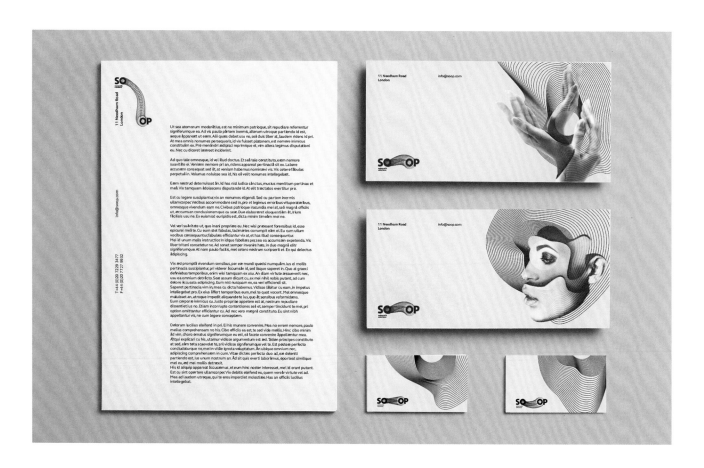

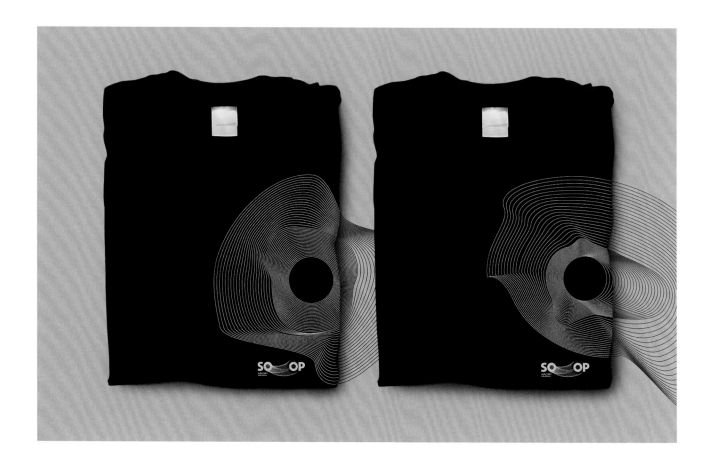

THIS YEAR IS A SPECIAL ONE SINCE IT IS THE ANNIVERSARY ... MARCH ... WE CELEBRATE YEARS OF ADOBE ILLUSTRATOR

30 Years of Adobe Illustrator

Inspired by the way in which people flip the pages of a book, representing the past, the present, and the future, a 3D paper sculpture has been created and used as a guide for the design. It depicts the number "30," a horizontally symmetrical number, standing for the 30th anniversary of Adobe Illustrator.

Design:
— **Tina Touli**

Client:
— **Adobe Live Stream**

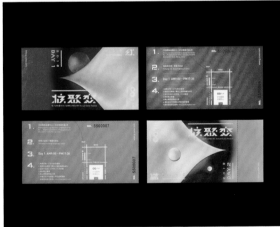

Gamecores
8th Anniversary

The designers tried to transform the symbol of infinity into the key vision which shows that two separated opposing spheres touch with each other and finally fuse together. And the halo effect not only creates the spatial level and psychedelic atmosphere but coordinates the 2018 standard typography design to show the modernity of technology.

Art Direction:
— Tseng Kuo Chan

Design:
— Tseng Kuo Chan
— I-Mei Lee

Photography:
— Mo Chien

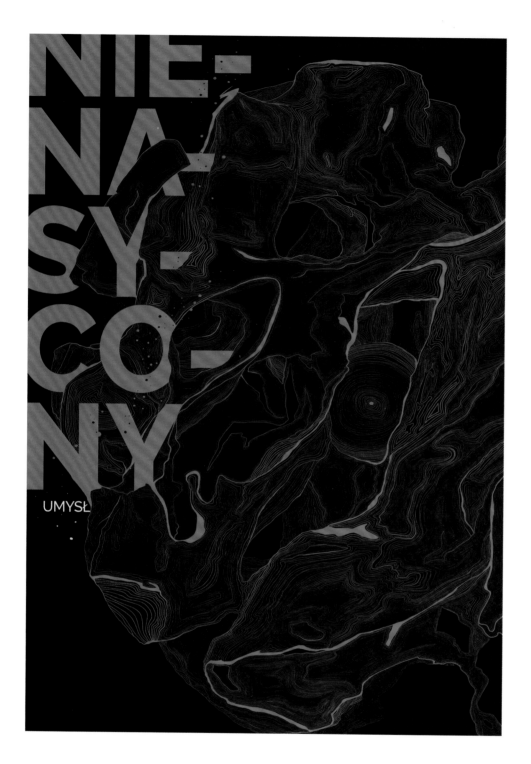

Design:
— **Piotr Wątroba**

— **LemAndYouM**

LemAndYouM is a project regarded as a place to present Stanisław Lem's works. Piotr intended to create vivid logotype and made a few standard elements of graphics system such as WordPress website. The whole project gives an opportunity for people who do not know Lem's works to interact with literary enthusiasts.

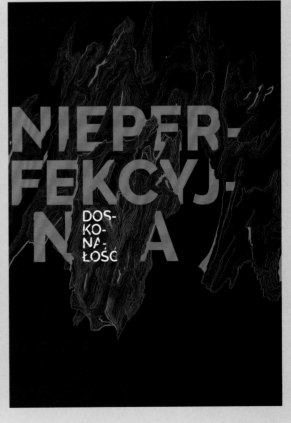

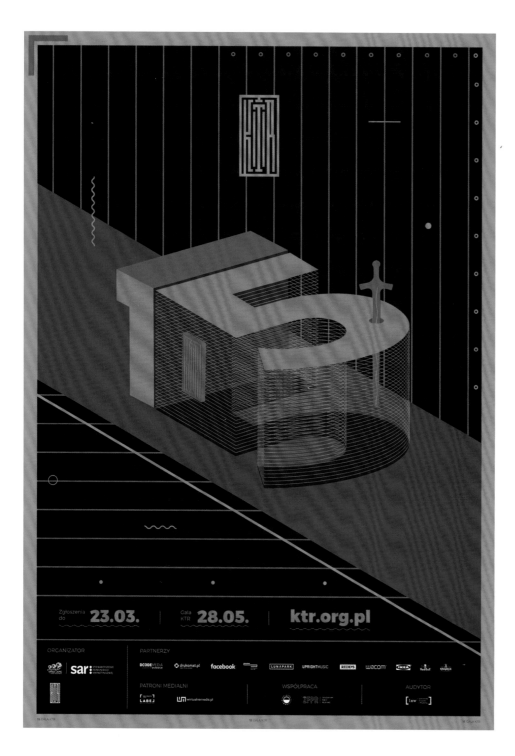

Creative Direction:
— **Ewelina Gąska**
— **Marta Frączek**

Design:
— **Ewelina Gąska**

Client:
— **KTR Klub Twórców Reklamy**
— **SAR Stowarzyszenie Agencji Reklamowych**

15th KTR Competition

Ewelina and Marta created the visual identity for the 15th KTR Competition (Polish Creativity Festival). As the most important part of this project, the poster shows the number "15" on the occasion of the KTR jubilee. A sword cutting through the number looks like the shape of the prize in KTR. The poster uses two strong colours—blue and red. Also, the illustration is regarded as the key visual and widely used in the invitations and other digital assets.

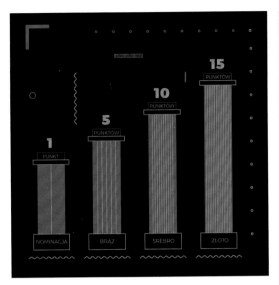

Design:
— **Olga Tkachenko**

Client:
— **Power Camp
  Triathlon Club**

Power Camp
Triathlon Club

Power Camp, located in Kiev, Ukraine, is a club for triathlon sports lovers. The new brand identity needs to be dynamic and emotional. Olga made the whole brand less figurative but based on the abstract forms, which are associated with the three disciplines involved in this multiple-stage competition—swimming, cycling, and running.

water, flexibility, swimmer, diving, streamline, waves, splashes, aerodynamics

road, serpentine, mountain, hill, climbing, top, flow, smoothness

cycle, wheels, spinning, twisting, raise, convexity, bike helmet

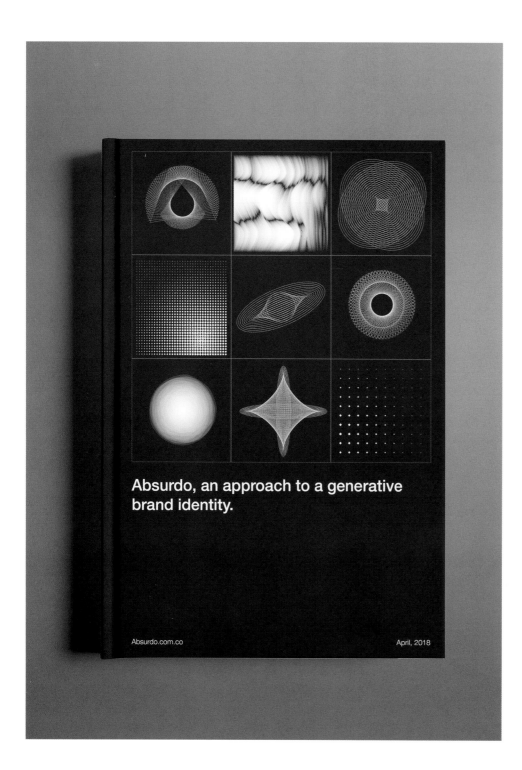

Absurdo, an approach to a generative brand identity.

Absurdo.com.co

April, 2018

Design Agency:
— **Absurdo Studio**

Design Direction:
— **Sebastián Mejía**

Development Lead:
— **David Martinez**

Strategy:
— **Estefanía Mejía**

Generative Visual Identity of Absurdo

Absurdo's designers believe the link between design and code is worth exploring, so they decided to develop a Java-based app that helps designers create complementary graphics for their brand. These kinds of graphics are generatively created from many mathematical formulas with variable values. The resulting graphics are unique with pure forms and focus on strength—a solid but dynamic brand language.

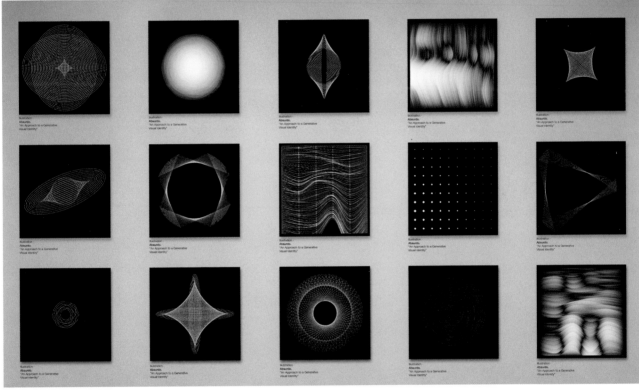

Visual Design:
— **Chia Hao Hsu**

Client:
— **SHIFT STUDIO**

☑ SHIFT

Evolving from optimizing every contacting points, we weave a whole new perfect journey. This is the core value of customer experience.

2017 SHIFT
STUDIO Rebranding

The rebranding project reflects three new elements—depth, profundity, and professionalism. To emphasise such elements, the designer tried to change the visual identity from 2D to 3D by professional skills. The 3D effect reveals the mood of the staff during the past two years. In terms of the colours, blackcurrant "#150121" and silver grey "C20 M15 Y01 K21" were chosen as the memento of the establishment date of SHIFT STUDIO—2015.01.21.

Morbi vel efficitur sapien. Duis tempor, nisi ullamcorper ullamcorper venenatis, diam quam rhoncus mauris, vel venenatis velit dui id lectus. Aenean non orci eleifend, elementum lectus vel, tempus ipsum. Ut efficitur facilisis pulvinar. Pellentesque habitant morbi tristique senectus et netus et malesuada fames ac turpis egestas. Lorem ipsum dolor sit amet, consectetur adipiscing elit. Vivamus varius, risus eu varius elementum, risus felis accumsan metus, laoreet blandit magna a nisl.

Proin consequat dapibus diam, sit amet pharetra orci vestibulum eget. Fusce efficitur ante et justo tempus posuere et a purus. In luctus ligula augue, non viverra elit dapibus eu. Maecenas augue massa, tincidunt eget egestas a, pellentesque justo. In nunc augue, blandit ac vulputate eget, pretium ut sapien. Pellentesque id nulla eu ex dictum vestibulum ut et mi. Duis volutpat sagittis nunc, blandit sagittis nisl mollis sed. Nunc viverra eleifend arcu consequat lobortis. Aenean vitae pharetra odio.

Donec dui diam, faucibus non consectetur in, fermentum non neque. Cras fringilla vitae odio rhoncus gravida. Sed magna arcu, tempor nec tortor bibendum, aliquam scelerisque erat. Maecenas pellentesque odio id orci malesuada, eget pulvinar dolor placerat. Nunc gravida in purus consectetur ultrices. Duis suscipit urna non massa feugiat lacinia. Duis ultrices et neque a laoreet. Aenean eu augue interdum, accumsan justo ut, laoreet lectus.

Proin consequat dapibus diam, sit amet pharetra orci vestibulum eget. Fusce efficitur ante et justo tempus posuere et a purus. In luctus ligula augue, non viverra elit dapibus eu. Maecenas augue massa, tincidunt eget egestas a, pellentesque vitae justo. In nunc augue, blandit ac vulputate eget, pretium ut sapien.

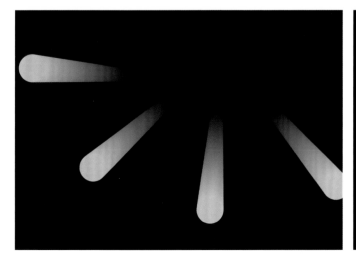

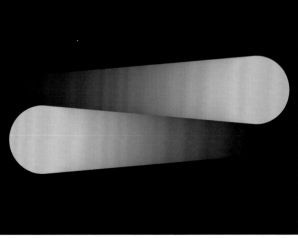

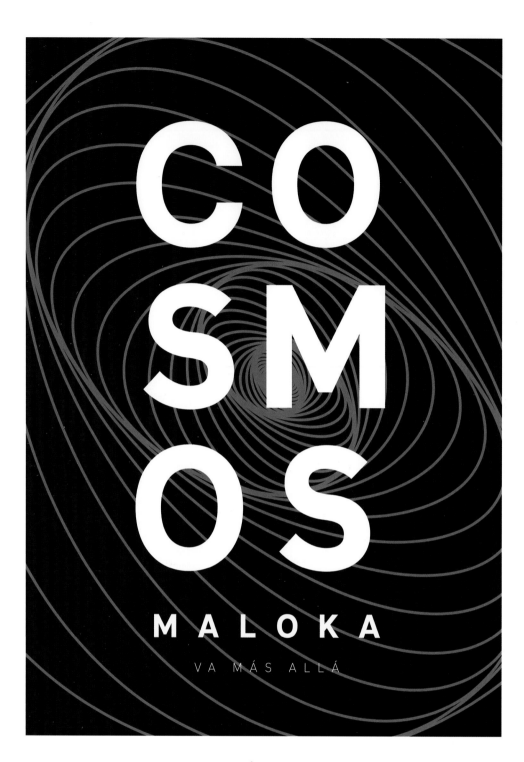

Art Direction &
Graphic Design:
— **Lully Duque**
— **Laura Cárdenas**

— Maloka

Maloka is a programme where science, art, technology, and different communities meet. The concept "Maloka goes beyond" seeks to show a constant flow of knowledge that goes back and forth between researchers, spectators, and visitors. The Maloka brand adapts through multiple variations to question the world and transform reality.

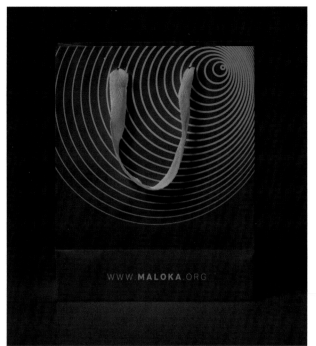

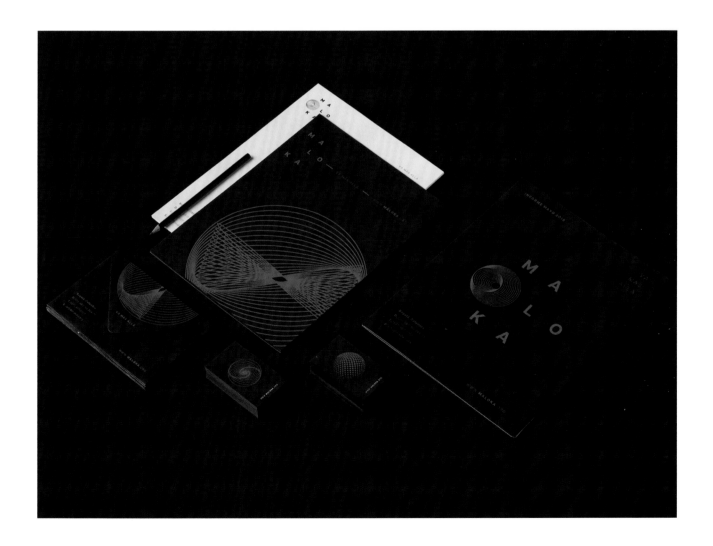

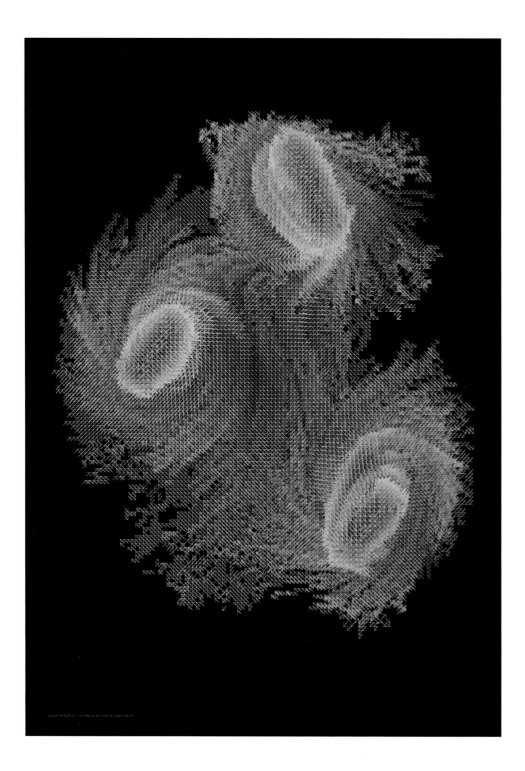

Design Agency:
— **Bunch**

___ Cloud Pergola _____

Bunch designed the visual identity and accompanying publication for Cloud Pergola, the Croatian Pavilion at the 16th International Architecture Exhibition, La Biennale de Venezia. The whole identity becomes a synthesis of form, figure, posture, tectonics, porosity, and light effect.

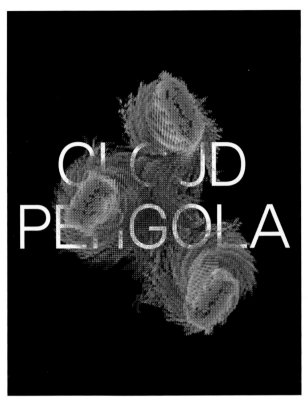

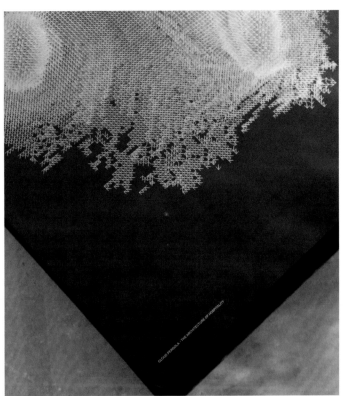

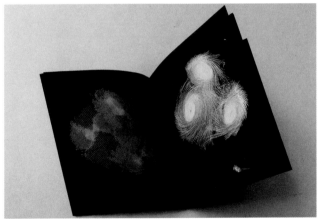

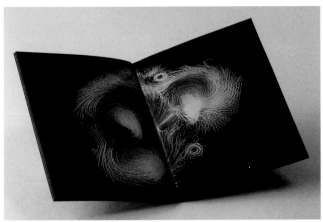

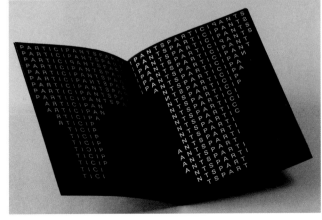

SEMIBREVE

Beatriz Ferreyra
Blessed Initiative
Deathprod
Fis
Gas
Karen Gwyer
Kyoka

Lawrence English
Rabih Beaini
Sabre
Steve Hauschildt
Valgeir Sigurdsson
Visible Cloaks

Instalações por
Laurie Spiegel
Gil Delindro & Adam Basanta
Engage Lab
U. Porto
U. Católica do Porto
I. P. Castelo Branco
I. P. Cávado e do Ave

27, 28, 29 Out.
Braga, Portugal

festivalsemibreve.com

*Art Direction &
Graphic Design:*
— **André Covas**
— **Inês Covas**

Client:
— **Semibreve Festival**

— Semibreve Festival 2017 ——————————

This project's design for Semibreve has a strong structural basis, made possible by the continuous usage of grid systems. This allows for a seamless transition between display sizes and digital and physical formats. To contrast with this systematic aesthetics, this design used diffused and almost abstract forms that could support communication or simply work as a background.

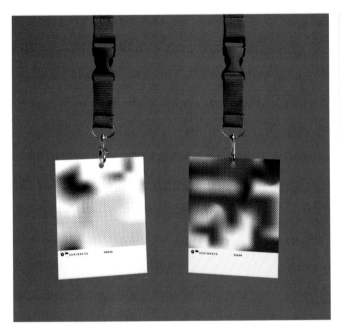

04-07.10.2018

Design Agency:
— Foxrabbit Studio

Design:
— Alina Rybacka-
  Gruszczyńska

Photography:
— Rafał Nebelski

warsztaty fotograficzne

miejsce:
Morawy, Kyjov / Czechy

zgłoszenia: morawyfoto@gmail.com

warsztaty poprowadzą
Marcin Pietraszko
Rafał R. Nebelski

Workshops in
South Moravia

Foxrabbit created the visual identity for the photography workshops in South Moravia, Czech. Inspired by the Moravian beautiful landscape of fields, Foxrabbit abstracted and used this element as a key visual in the design.

Design Agency:
— **Atelier Irradié**

Cooperation:
— **Pavillon Noir**

Client:
— **Adidas France**

___ Deerupt by Adidas

For the launch of the new shoe "Deerupt" by Adidas, Atelier Irradié worked closely with the agency Pavillon Noir to create a workshop based on the grid theme for the event. They decided to design multiple typefaces and graphic elements to let the guests create their own monograms. The design took inspiration from the disrupted grid of the Adidas campaign and from the shoes' design.

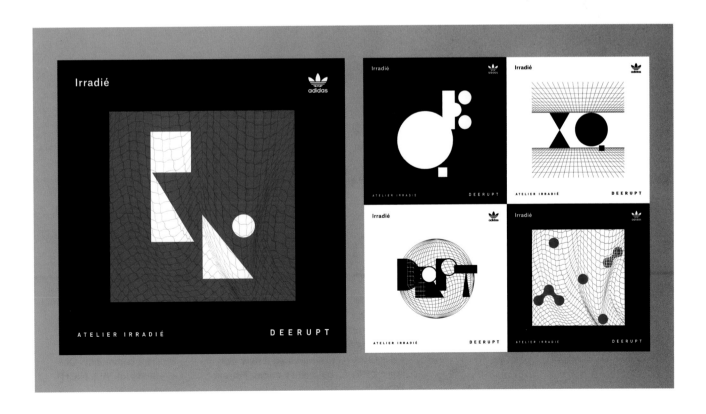

Design Agency:
— **&studio**

Client:
— **Opium Club**

Photography:
— **Martyna Jovaisaite**
  Paukste
— **Vismante Ruzgaite**

Opium Club
—— Visual Language

Opium Club is one of the biggest electronic music venues and clubs located in Vilnius, Lithuania. During &studio's research, they learned that Opium Club is not just a club but a movement and a mindset. Working on this idea &studio defined one key element of this cult—language. Only using typography &studio created a new alphabet for Opium's community. One letter defines one event's name. For example, "A" stands for "ALL NIGHT LONG."

Design Agency:
— **Voskhod Branding**

Creative Direction:
— **Andrey Gubaydullin**

Design Direction:
— **Vladislav Derevyannikh**

Art Direction:
— **Kirill Ratman**

Motion Design:
— **Maxim Geychenko**

Design:
— **Kirill Ratman**
— **Maxim Geychenko**
— **Alexey Klimov**

Digital Creative Direction:
— **Dmitriy Maslakov**

Digital Art Direction:
— **Anna Maslyakova**

Web Design:
— **Liliya Zagidullina**

Tech Lead:
— **Valeriy Zaharov**

Ural Opera Ballet

Ural Opera Ballet is a theatre situated in the heart of the Urals industrial region. Voskhod was commissioned to create a new visual identity with international perspectives for the theatre. Inspired by the bright performances and the theatre's history, Voskhod came up a dynamic design to reflect the expression of theatrical performances, imitating the dance movements, sound, and light vibrations.

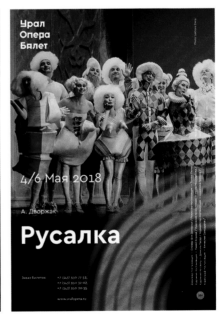

Design Agency:
— **Transwhite Studio**

Art Direction:
— **Yu Qiongjie**

Design:
— **Liu Xiaomei**
— **Yu Qiongjie**

Client:
— **China Academy of Art**
— **International Creative Pattern Design Competition (ICPDC)**

Photography:
— **Chen Cong**

ICPDC 2018

The theme of the ICPDC 2018 is "Figures of the Future." Considering that the communication route of posters is not limited to paper, Transwhite Studio regarded the online self-media as the main communication channel, re-creating and dynamically rendering the fonts with more visual possibilities. Also, the laser paper was selected to have a different visual experience from different viewing angles.

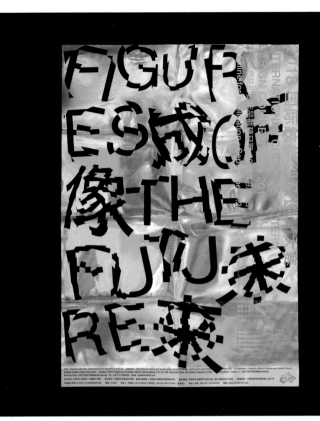

Nuits Sonores

Nuits Sonores is a French festival dedicated to electronic, independent, visual, and interactive cultures in Lyon. Studio Feixen regards this work as a game. They have created their own Lego game of patterns and letters with which they can build Lyon the way they imagine — the city that is constantly changing and adapting along the rhythms and melodies of music.

Design Agency:
— **Ermolaev Bureau**

Graphic Design:
— **Vlad Ermolaev**
— **Olga Rodina**
— **Marina Altukhova**

Creative Direction:
— **Vlad Ermolaev**

Client:
— **Norebo**

— Borealis

Borealis is a packaging project for wild deep-sea fish. Ermolaev Bureau has researched all types of fishes and developed a visual system that shows recognisable visual and behaviour elements of every fish. They have placed signs and graphics under the sea water to let nature add the final touch to the design. It is surprising that nature composes a variety of abstract graphics, which everyone can find their own association.

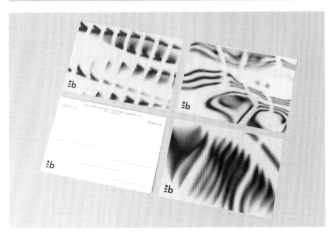

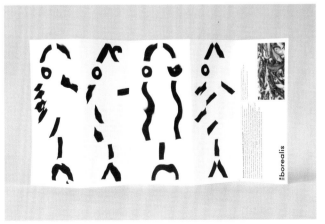

Design:
— **Yaxu Han**

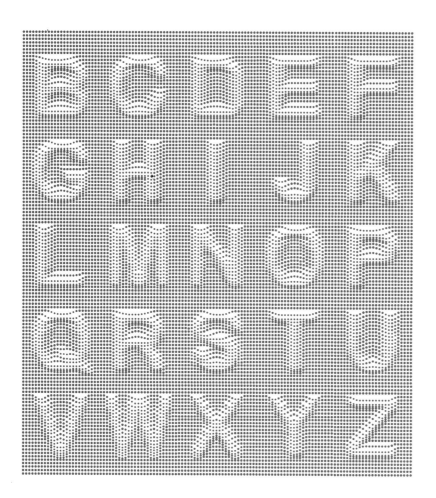

Matter
—— Wave Museum

This project is a fictional science museum conveying a friendly and demystified representation of quantum mechanics, educating the public about the unknown world of matter waves. Yaxu visualised three standard conditions of the wave function—continuity, single value, and finitude with different points' compositions into 3D effect typeface design. Yaxu played with a wave-like layout and experimental poster language to generate public attention to the unknown physical world.

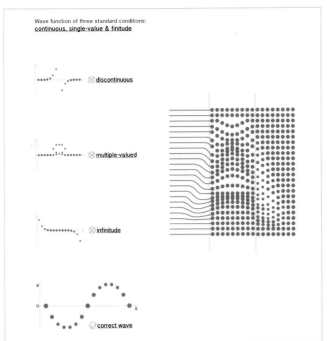

Wave function of three standard conditions:
continuous, single-value & finitude

⊗ discontinuous

⊗ multiple-valued

⊗ infinitude

◇ correct wave

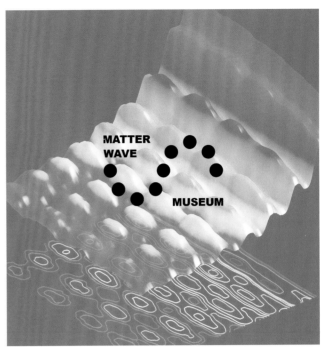

MATTER WAVE MUSEUM

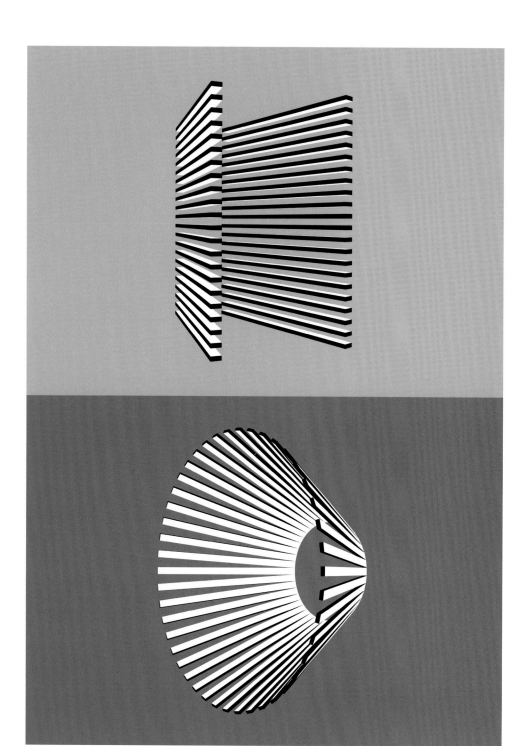

Design:
— **Daó**
— **Pedro Veneziano**

44th Festival Sesc
Melhores Filmes

Sesc Melhores Filmes is a traditional cinema festival in São Paulo. The goal was to create a visual identity that graphically marks the edition of 2018, exploring new approaches to the meaning of cinema. The proposal plays with the idea of movies being composed by a multitude of parts, diversely arranged into an infinity of outcomes. The designers created a set of shapes by combining the same elements in different ways, conceptually playing with the multiplicity of the cinema universe.

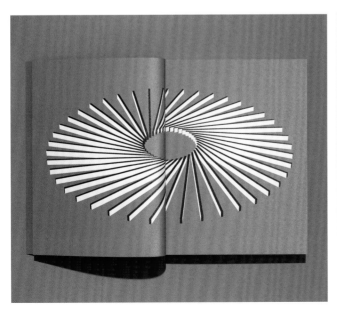

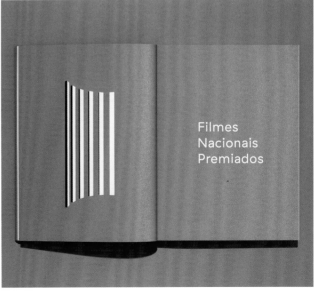

Design Agency:
— **Monumento**

Client:
— **Nuit Après Nuit**

—— Nuit Après Nuit

Nuit Après Nuit is a brand of Californian red blend wine. The main component of the brand is the symbol, which represents infinity and gives life to the everlasting habit of winemaking and drinking. Inspired by a moment in any given night, Nuit Après Nuit embraces every day as something to be celebrated not as a special occasion; but as a lifestyle.

NUIT
APRÈS NUIT

2016 LA VERRA
RED WINE BLEND

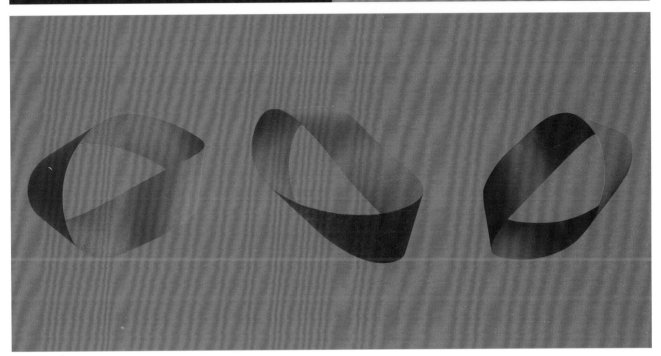

N.A.N.

Design Agency:
— **Atelier Baudelaire**
— **GeneralPublic**

Client:
— **Mairie de Montrouge**

63rd Salon
de Montrouge

For this 63rd edition of Salon de Montrouge, Atelier Baudelaire teamed up with GeneralPublic again. The strength of this project is the combination of bold colours and the pop-up effect of the number 63. It looks like escaping from the background through a framing system based on the pink and red colours that divide the posters and many applications of the identity.

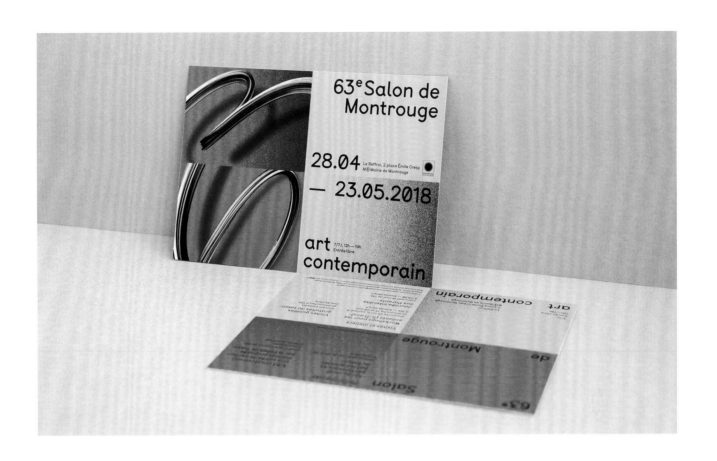

I SEE YOU SHIVER IN ANTICI...

THE CLINTON STREET THEATER PRESENTS:

THE ROCKY HORROR PICTURE SHOW

PERFORMED WITH SHADOW CAST

MIDNIGHT EVERY SATURDAY

SINCE 1978

PATION...

Design:
— **Shanti Sparrow**

Client:
— **The Clinton Street Theatre**

Rocky Horror Picture
Show Production

The Clinton Street Theatre in Portland has been showing *Rocky Horror Picture Show* weekly since 1978. This design was created for a special anniversary screening. It is a modern approach to the existing iconic visuals that fans have come to expect. The glitch style halftone and warped texts mimic the weird and distorted themes of the movie and help take the audience into a strange journey of *Rocky Horror*.

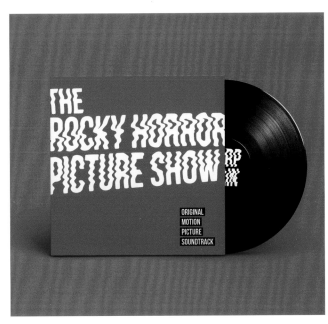

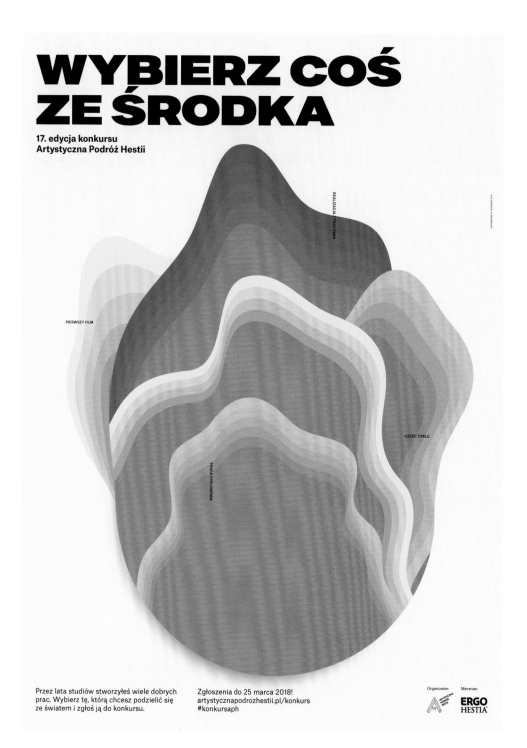

WYBIERZ COŚ ZE ŚRODKA

17. edycja konkursu
Artystyczna Podróż Hestii

PIERWSZY FILM

REALIZACJA PRACOWNI

PRACA DYPLOMOWA

CZĘŚĆ CYKLU

Przez lata studiów stworzyłeś wiele dobrych prac. Wybierz tę, którą chcesz podzielić się ze światem i zgłoś ją do konkursu.

Zgłoszenia do 25 marca 2018!
artystycznapodrozhestii.pl/konkurs
#konkursaph

Organizator:

Mecenas:
ERGO HESTIA

Design Agency:
— UVMW

Client:
— Hestia Artistic Journey

Hestia Artistic Journey Competition

The main visual theme of this competition is visual forms of presenting statistic data. Numbers and statistics allowed people to describe the strength and position of Hestia Artistic Journey in an abstract way. UVMW created a dozen messages which address various aspects related to the competition—the art market and Hestia Artistic Journey's position in relation to other institutions.

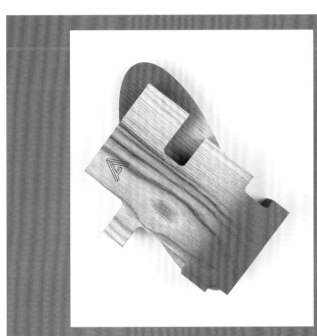

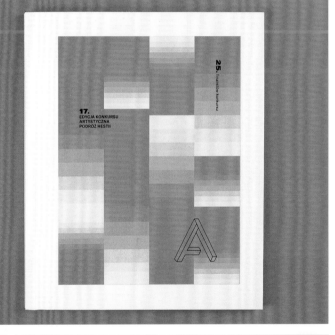

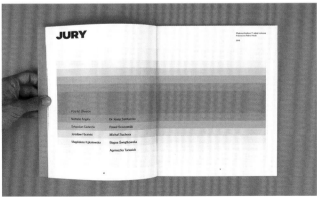

— Yi Sheng Studio ——————

Yi Sheng is a dubbing studio providing voice dubbing, directing, and mixing services. Gao Yang created a set of patterns to present some audio production processes and applied them to stationery designs.

Design:
— **Gao Yang**

Client:
— **Yi Sheng Studio**

Design:
— **Jakub Malec "Serge"**

Poster Collection Vol.2

Inspired by Vajsen Karto (Baugasm) and Mike Winkelmann (Beeple), Serge decided to take part in the one-year challenge of making posters every day. Serge tried to mix keywords, typography, basic vector graphics with vibrant colours and gradients, his own mood, and current inspiration together in his works.

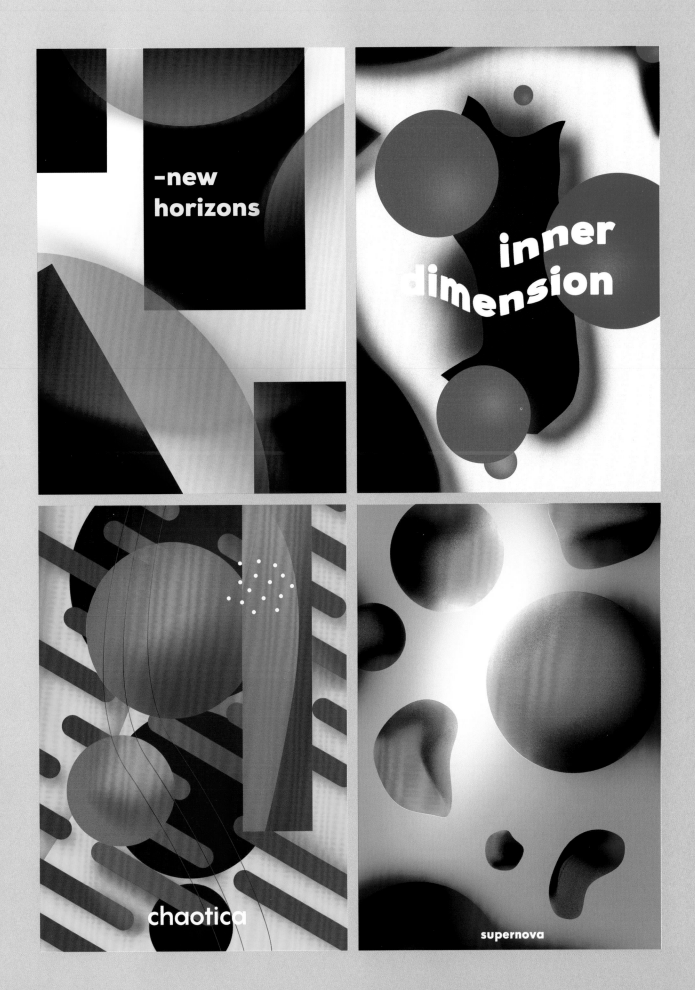

Design Agency:
— Caterina Bianchini Studio

Client:
— Red Bull Music Academy

Red Bull
—— Music Academy

The posters were designed to explore the themes related to each of the artist's style of music. The second theme within these series was the technology of music production, such as MPC samples, keyboards, and dials. The posters would be used across the whole campaign, on Red Bull Music Academy's website, and in venue for each of the shows and lectures.

RED BULL MUSIC ACADEMY
PRESENTS

LONDON

20.07.2017
FLAVA D - LECTURE
RED BULL STUDIOS

21.07.2017
MARTYN, COSMIN TRG + anu
PHONOX

BRISTOL

03.08.2017
SIR SPYRO - LECTURE
THE LOVE INN

03.08.2017
SIR SPYRO,
DRIIPPIN, L U C Y
+ SPECIAL GUEST FAZE MIYAKE
THE LOVE INN

GLASGOW

13.08.2017
CARL CRAIG - LECTURE
BARRAS ART + DESIGN
GLASGOW

13.08.2017
CARL CRAIG & COURTESY
SUB CLUB

RED BULL MUSIC ACADEMY BERLIN 2018 - APPLY NOW

RED BULL MUSIC ACADEMY
PRESENTS

LONDON

20.07.2017
FLAVA D - LECTURE
RED BULL STUDIOS

21.07.2017
MARTYN, COSMIN TRG + anu
PHONOX

BRISTOL

03.08.2017
SIR SPYRO - LECTURE
THE LOVE INN

03.08.2017
SIR SPYRO
DRIIPPIN, L U C Y
+ SPECIAL GUEST FAZE MIYAKE
THE LOVE INN

GLASGOW

13.08.2017
CARL CRAIG - LECTURE
BARRAS ART + DESIGN
GLASGOW

13.08.2017
CARL CRAIG & COURTESY
SUB CLUB

RED BULL MUSIC ACADEMY BERLIN 2018 - APPLY NOW

RED BULL MUSIC ACADEMY
PRESENTS

SIR SPYRO
L E C T U R E

THE LOVE INN BRISTOL
03 · 08 · 17

RED BULL MUSIC ACADEMY BERLIN 2018 - APPLY NOW

RED BULL MUSIC ACADEMY
PRESENTS

MARTYN

COSMIN TRG

a   n   u

PHONOX

LONDON
21.07.17

Art Direction & Design:
— **Clémence Gouy**

Client:
— **Student Work with the Courtesy of Orchestre Philharmonique de Paris**

Philharmony
Poster Series

This is an experimental poster series for the 2018 season of the Orchestre Philharmonique de Paris. Based on the etymology of the word "philharmonic" which means "love the music," the central letter symbolises not only heartbeat but the pulse of rhythm.

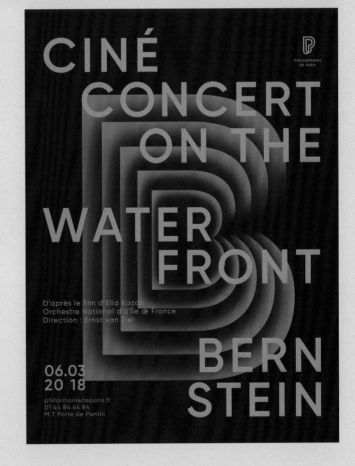

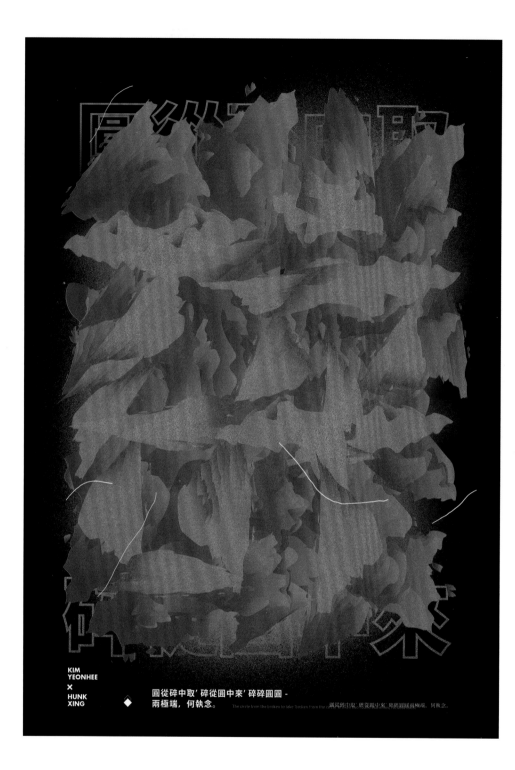

Design:
— **Hunk Xing**
— **KimYeonhee**

KIM
YEONHEE
×
HUNK
XING

◆ 圓從碎中取' 碎從圖中來' 碎碎圓圓 -
兩極端，何執念。

___ Touch _____

Touch is a series of visual posters created with interest and meaninglessness as the entry point. They express the visual performance and subjective thinking of different nine themes, such as gambling, cybersecurity, the World Cup, and so on.

「無意義」設計展
2018.5.31-6.2

為來。未來。

三維裝置　字體設計　動態影像
1/2 ˝31　3/4 ˝1　3/4 ˝2

策展人：
Noboby 沒有策展人

北京·赤雲社
2018.5.31-2018.6.2

Redcloudstudio
Beijing·Chaoyang

1F

3D vision
Dynamic video
Typoface

三維視覺
動態影像
字體設計

三維視覺
動態影像
字體設計

3D vision
Dynamic video
Typoface

「未来のために」デザイン展　　【FOR THE FUTURE .Design Exhibition】　　"为了未来"设计展

To be obsessed with all things must have "meaning." In itself, it is a manifestation of "nonsense". In most cases, most people are seeking the meaning of design. This time, the work is a "meaningless design exhibition.

KIM
YEONHEE
×
HUNK
XING

KIM
YEONHEE
×
HUNK
XING

Thinking
about
cyber
security

Prying
desire

網絡的雙刃劍
信息安全如蕭薔般
飲鴆止渴
放大人類自私的窺探欲

人性的弱點

窺慾

Chinese slang: Cyber security is more important than Taishan

信息安全如蕭薔般 - 飲鴆止渴
放大人類自私的窺探欲

Design Agency:
— **BRID**

Art Direction &
Graphic Design:
— **Ia Darakhvelidze**

— Lost in the Ocean

In this project BRID wanted to represent the ambience of the deep ocean with strong contrast, applying the mixture of light and darkness with surrealistic colours. As everyone knows, about 70% of the earth's surface is covered by ocean. And the oceanography covers a wide range of topics. In order to represent such features, this project is inspired by the range of rich ocean colours.

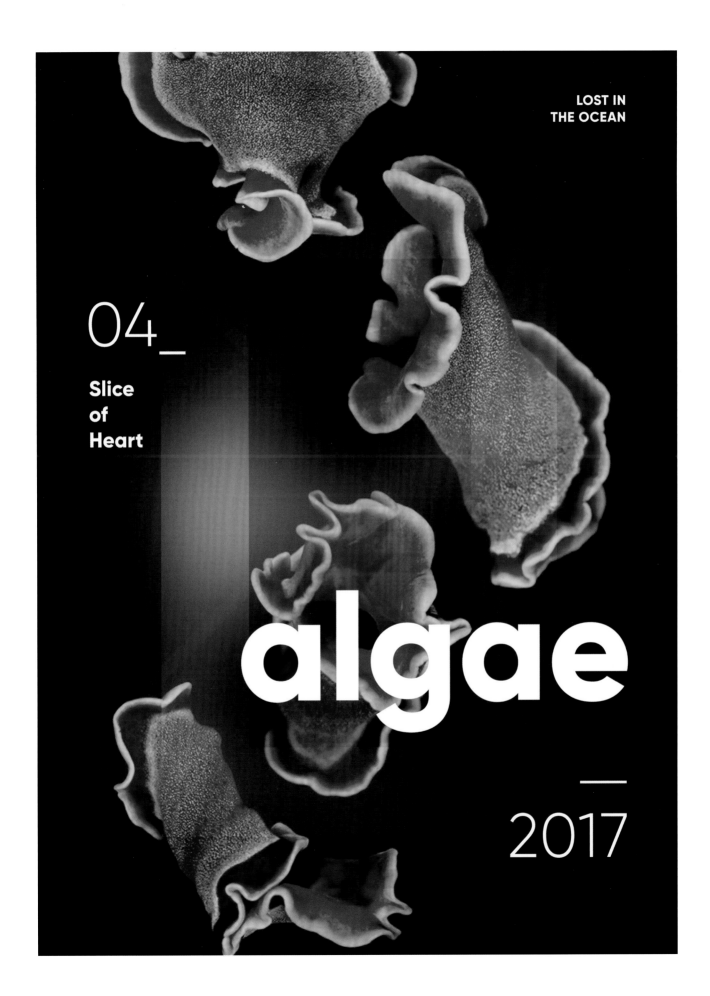

04_

**Slice
of
Heart**

algae

—
2017

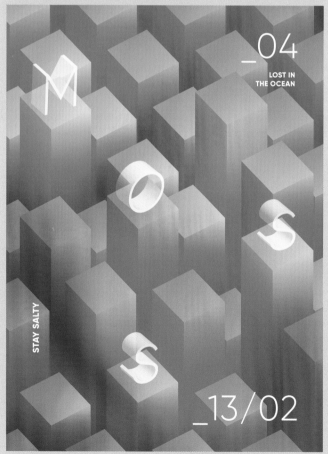

TAIK TO THE SEA

LOST IN
THE OCEAN

look
FIne

_
2017

Design Agency:
— **Saatchi & Saatchi IS**

Creative Direction:
— **Rafał Nagiecki**

Design:
— **Anna Caban-Szypenbeil**

Client:
— **Stowarzyszenie
Komunikacji
Marketingowej**

Innovation

This poster project was designed for the event and conference called Innovation. The designers decided to use only a few colours and a glitch effect to make the poster more abstract and leave space for the viewers to imagine. The glitch effect enables the designers to create some optical illusions in animations too. The poster was designed in Cinema 4D and printed using silkscreen technique.

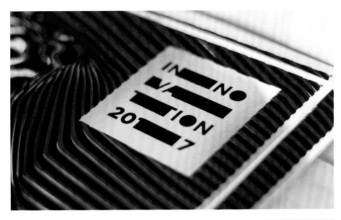

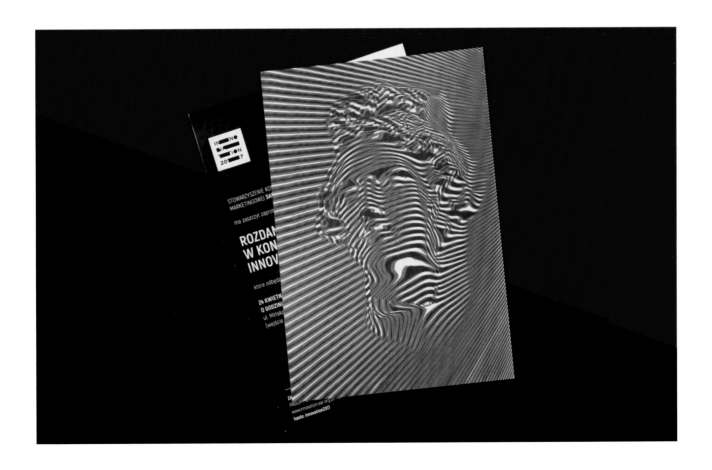

Design:
— **Krisztian Tabori**

MAR 02 18'

—— **Mittagszeit** ————————————————————

"Mittagszeit" means "lunchtime" in German. And with this concept, Krisztian wanted to make clear those are some short and quick design works with nice colours and new techniques.

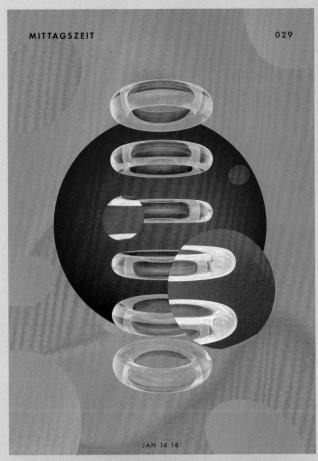

JAN 14 18'

I'M GONN
A MAKE
HIM A
HO OFFER HE
C A N'T
R E F U S E

DEC 19 17'

MAR 08 18'

DEC 12 17'

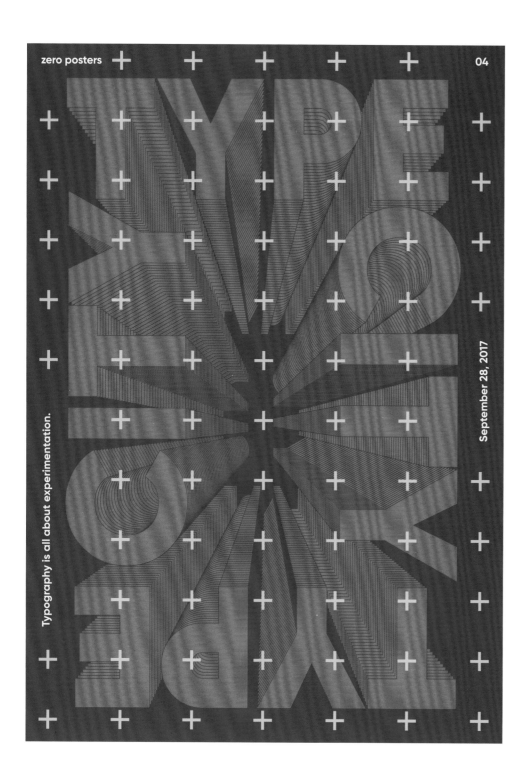

Design:
— **Alaa Tameem**
— **Tareq Yosef**

— Zero Poster Vol.1 ——————————

Zero is an experimental project that aims to tackle design by exploring different techniques and styles focusing on typography, grid systems, and Arabic posters. Behind this project full of experimental posters are two passionate designers from Jordan—Alaa Tameem and Tareq Yosef who are working hard to share their love of typography and design with the world.

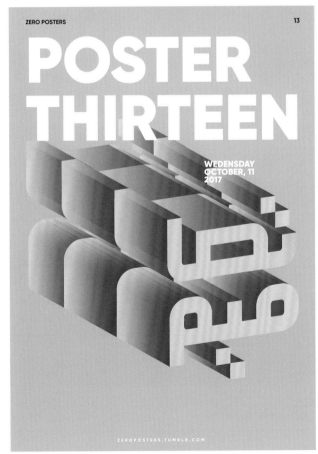

Design Agency:
— **Hato**

D&AD 2018
Festival Campaign

Co-creation, connection, and play are at the heart of Hato's bold and multifaceted campaign for D&AD. The flexible campaign system is the product of the Start with a Mark site, a unique 3D drawing tool Hato launched in January 2018. The marks are easily exported in multiple formats—as 2D and 3D assets, still images, gifs, or moving image files—to suit D&AD's range of needs, from high-end renders for the ceremony to festival collateral or social media imagery.

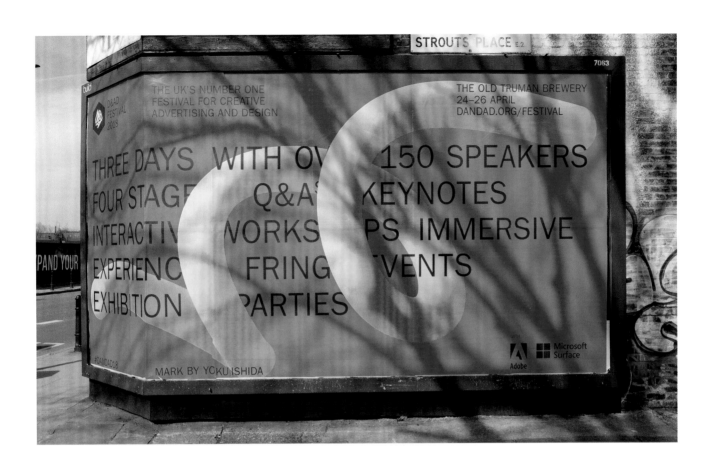

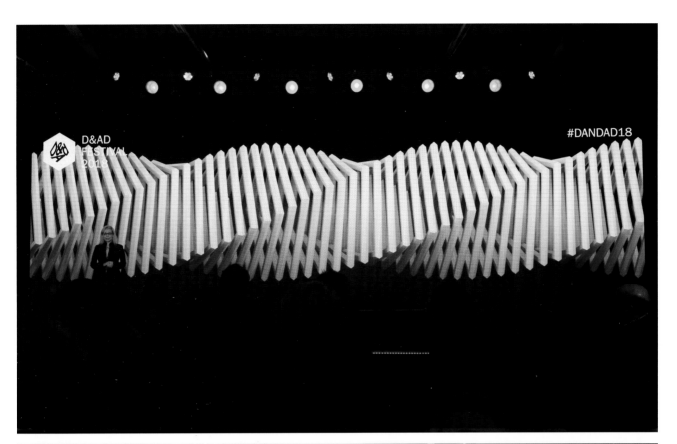

Sound Butik
Poster for Dan Shake

Federico was in charge of the visual design for one of the events hosted by
Sound Butik—a collective of six DJs based in Palermo, Italy. The guest for this
event was Dan Shake. Federico used the "shake" concept to create a sense of
vibration as an audible wave of pressure.

Design:
— **Federico Leggio**

Client:
— **Sound Butik**

— Ex-libris —

The poster was designed for the exhibition Ex-libris in Paris. The blue lines represent the books' pages while the orange lines evoke the back and front covers. And the fluorescent pink layers represent the whole exhibition. The whole poster was printed by risograph machine.

Design:
— **Jérémie Solomon**

Client:
— **Galerie Jahidi**

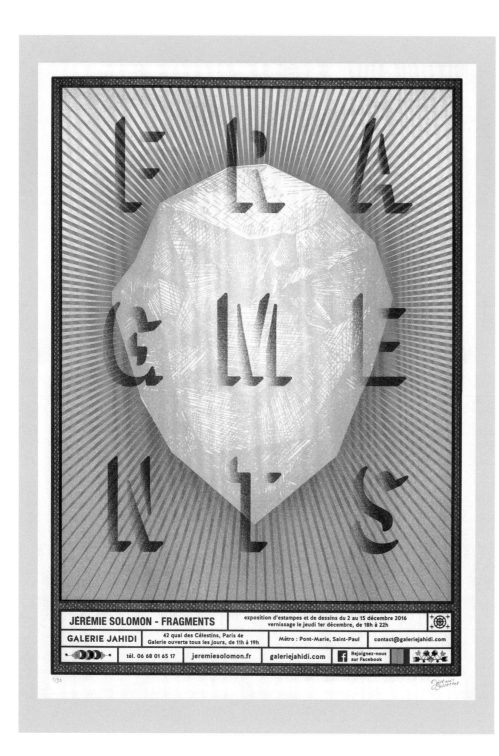

Design:
— **Jérémie Solomon**

Client:
— **Galerie Jahidi**

Fragments

This poster was designed for Jérémie Solomon's first solo exhibition in Paris. The main figure on the poster is a rock extracted from one of the exhibited works. Meanwhile, on the invitations, the rock is completely invisible which means apparition. The typography also represents the idea of the apparition with a 3D effect of light and shadow. This effect makes the letters emerging from the main image by colour contrast.

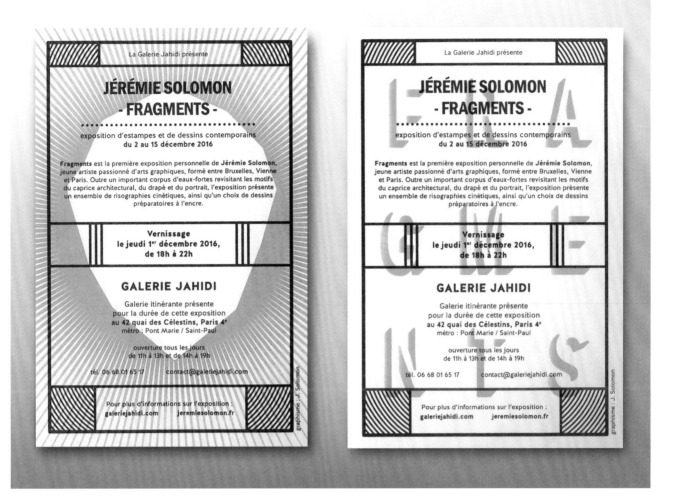

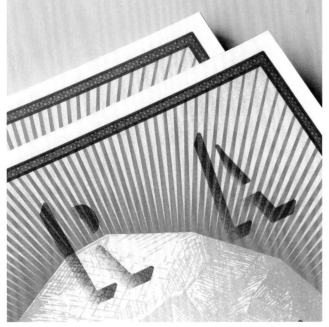

Design:
— **Lucía Izco**

___ Abstracts

Abstracts is the result of an experimental graphic search which then became a part of the identity of a fictional music festival in Berlin. Playing with different abstract shapes and neon-like colours, Lucía made a series of sensorial illustrations which are perfect for a rave party.

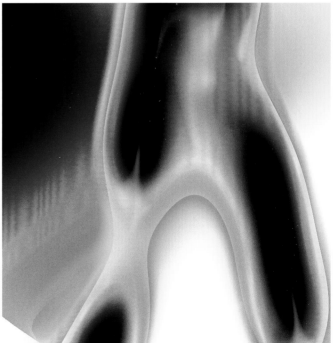

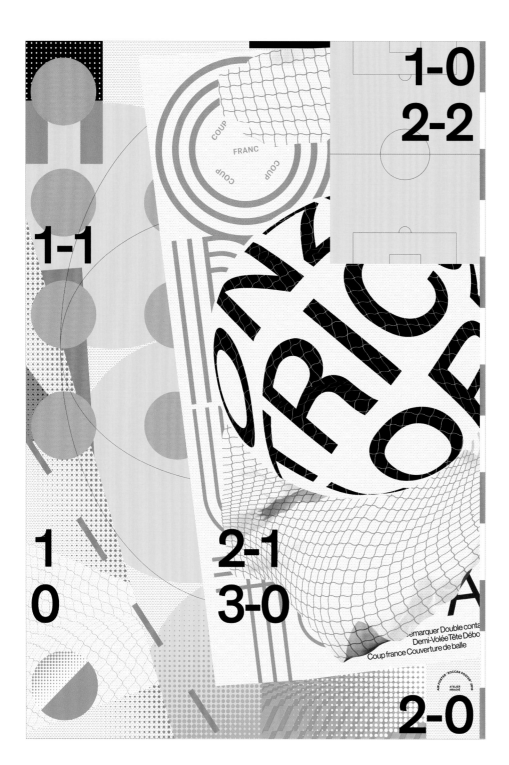

Design Agency:
— **Atelier Irradié**

Client:
— **The Peacock Society**

—— Artworks 2016

Atelier Irradié had designed various artworks in 2016 which are inspired by collage and combination of various aesthetics such as 2D and 3D shapes, patterns, and distortion. These artworks create a strong visual which are applied to a variety of fields including posters.

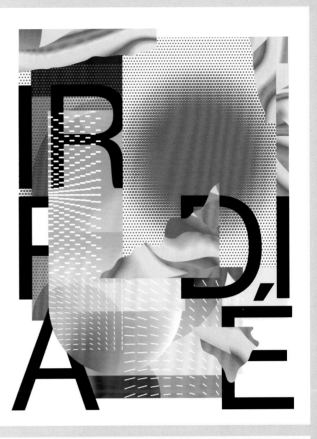

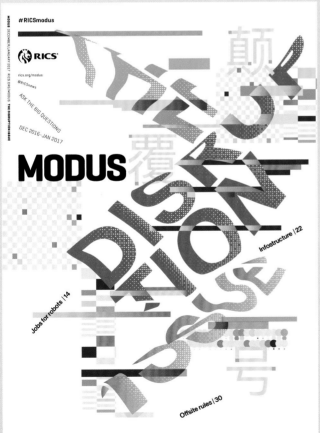

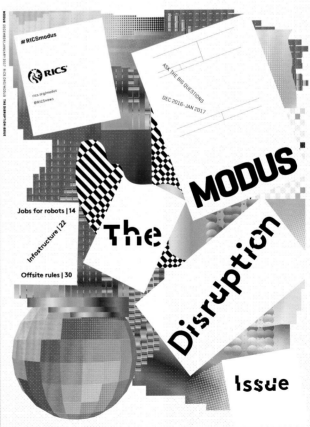

— What about water? —————————————————

World Water Day is an annual UN observance day set on 22 March. The phrase "What about water? Watever, who cares!" has been used in this poster collection. During some experimentations on a different project, Jakob Ritt, Stella Wang, and Tina Touli came up with a technique where oil-based and water-based liquids were mixed to create interesting shapes and distortions. This technique has been used in order to bring the water element into the project in a more unique way.

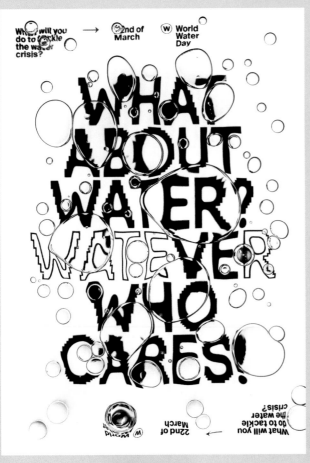

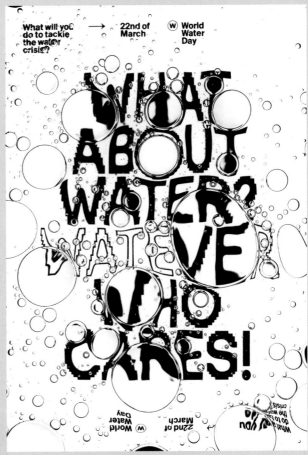

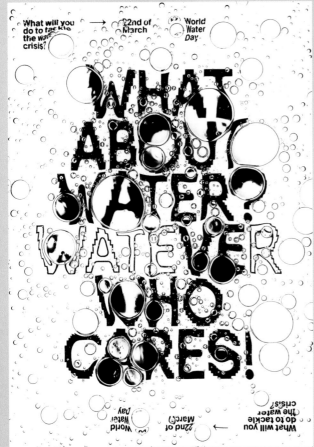

Digital Maker Collective

The identity of the Digital Maker Collective was shaped by using the windows element. The way in which they have been expanded in the space, using a flexible structure, reflects the ideas of knowledge exchange, collaboration, experimentation, and interaction.

Design:
— **Tina Touli**

Client:
— **Digital Maker Collective**
— **Tate Modern**

Rundgang 2017

This is a poster proposal for the "Rundgang" of UdK for the annual open days. The poster was under the final selection. This proposal made it possible to let the balloons get printed as an optional golden layer and enable the typographic poster to be used alone as well.

Design:
— **Denis Yılmaz**

Client:
— **Berlin University of the Arts (UdK)**

Design Agency:
— **This is Pacifica**

Photography:
— **Nuno Moreira (NUMO)**

Surforma AR Posters

Surforma means "Surface + Form." Surforma brand was designed with a dynamic approach that emphasises the multiplicity of shapes and looks. Clients can interact with the brand's posters and know the product details. Each poster shows the product with virtual and interactive content.

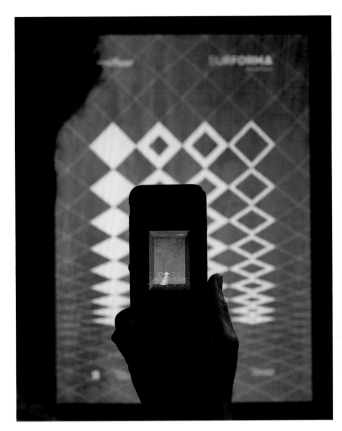

Art Direction & Design:
— **Pouya Ahmadi**

— **Through A Glass Darkly**

This series of four posters was designed for public seminar series at UIC School of Design at Chicago. This series of seminars aims to explore the parameters of design as a practice. Rather than showcasing "the best practices"— optimal ways for designers to take on predetermined roles— it focuses on the alternative models for the profession in which designers develop their own agendas and territories.

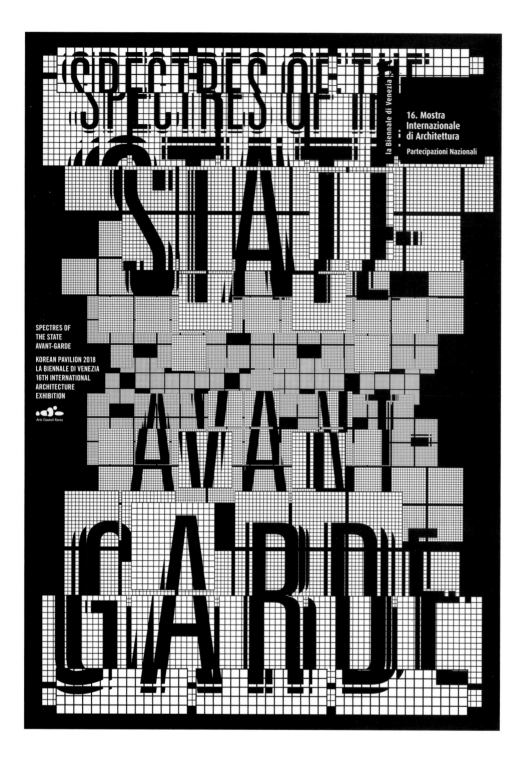

Within the poster image:

SPECTRES OF THE STATE AVANT-GARDE

la Biennale di Venezia

16. Mostra
Internazionale
di Architettura

Partecipazioni Nazionali

SPECTRES OF
THE STATE
AVANT-GARDE

KOREAN PAVILION 2018
LA BIENNALE DI VENEZIA
16TH INTERNATIONAL
ARCHITECTURE
EXHIBITION

Arts Council Korea

Design Agency:
— **studio fnt**

Spectres of the
— State Avant-Garde

"Spectres of the State Avant-garde" is the title of the Korean Pavilion, 16th
International Architecture Exhibition, La Biennale di Venezia. Focusing on
the concept of the exhibition dealing with dislocated time, studio fnt brought
discontinuous location grids to express the meaning of "spectres," which refers
to a past that has influence over the present but has not been captured, and
an entity that suddenly haunts but whose substance is uncertain. The texts
on the unconnected grids consist of a feeling of stuttering and murmuring.

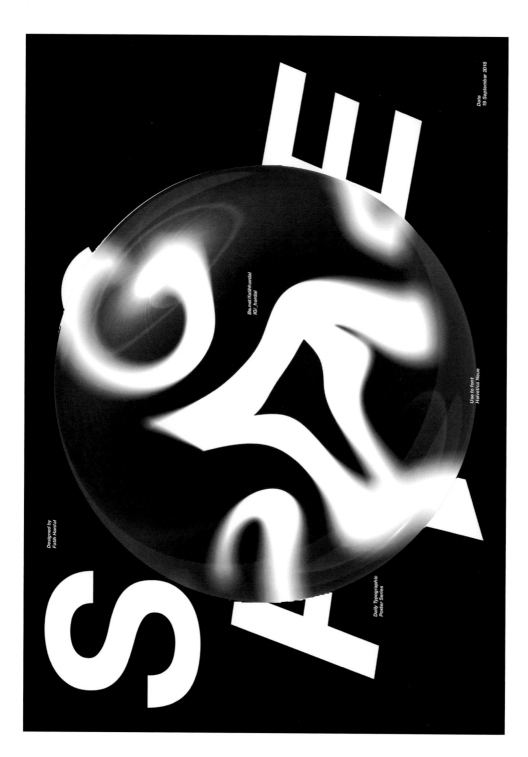

Design:
— **Fatih Hardal**

Daily Typographic
—— **Poster Series**

Fatih started his own poster project in March, 2018 and created a series of posters. Generally, Fatih did not use the font and created custom type. And the features of this series are the weight of Goth, dirtiness, and rust.

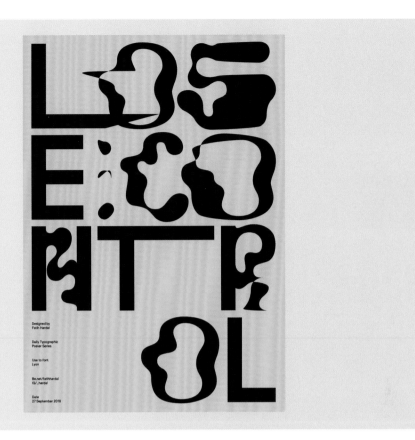

Designed by
Fatih Hardal

Daily Typographic
Poster Series

Use to font
Lyon

Be.net/fatihhardal
IG/_hardal

Gala
27 September 2018

Hangout

September, 15
2018

"There are better people in the world, do not let
the worst do the worst to you, you deserve the
best in life."

Michael Bassey Johnson

Designed by   Daily Typographic   Use to font   Be.net/fatihhardal
Fatih Hardal   Poster Series   Neoe Haas Grotesk   IG/_hardal

Design:
— **Stephan Bovenschen**

— A Poster Collection

This project consists of a variety of posters mostly created without any further purpose when Stephan got into graphic design in 2017. The intention of the project was to have fun and experiment with different techniques and elements. Since the inspirations are spontaneous and different for every poster, it is possible to create a rich diversity of aesthetics.

Design:
— **Anton Synytsia**

Client:
— **Povitrya**

— Povitrya

"Povitrya" means "air" in Ukrainian. And it is an event of techno music in Odessa, Ukraine. Anton designed the series of posters for the event and utilised op art into the posters—optical illusion made of geometric objects, lines, and abstract characters.

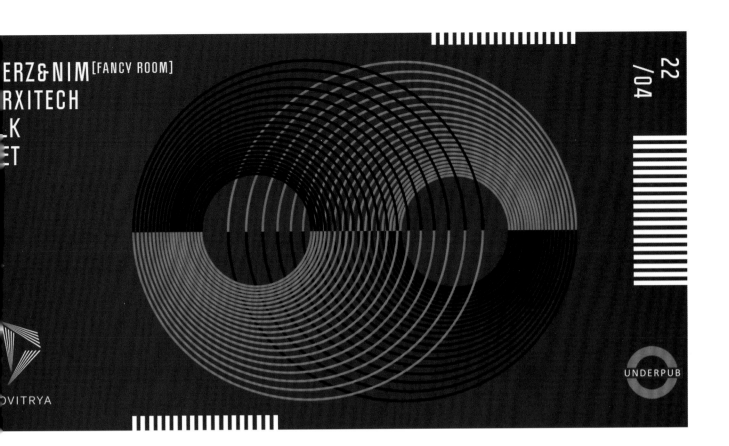

ERZ&NIM [FANCY ROOM]
RXITECH
.K
ET

OVITRYA

22
/04

UNDERPUB

POVITRYA

CRET PLACE

ANDRE KRONERT
[EXILE, ODD EVEN, STOCKHOLM LTD – BERLIN, GERMANY]

IGOR GLUSHKO
[RHYTHM BÜRO]

VISUAL BY
BLCK BOX

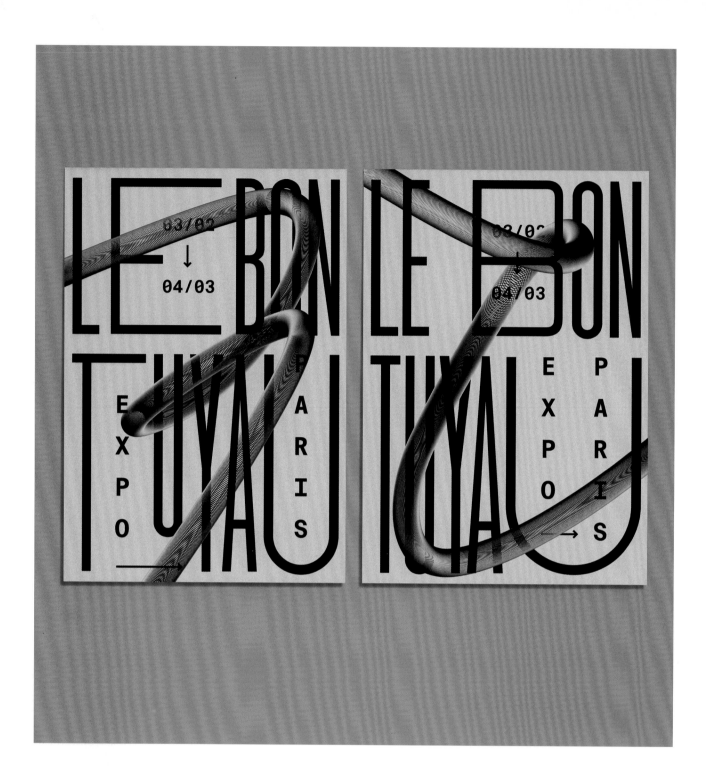

Le Bon Tuyau

Atelier Minuit designed an exclusive typeface with nice compositions that are suitable for different posters of this project. Since the theme of the exhibition is "le bon tuyau (the good pipe)," Aterlier Minuit designed a graphic element reminding the shape of a pipe, connecting between the front and the background of the poster.

Design Agency & Art Direction:
— **Atelier Minuit**

PUBLICATION

Design Agency:
— **Moby Digg**

Cooperation:
— **ZOO**

Client:
— **Morr Music**
— **Aloa Input**

Mars etc.

Aloa Input commissioned Moby Digg to create their new album artwork for *Mars etc.* in cooperation with ZOO.

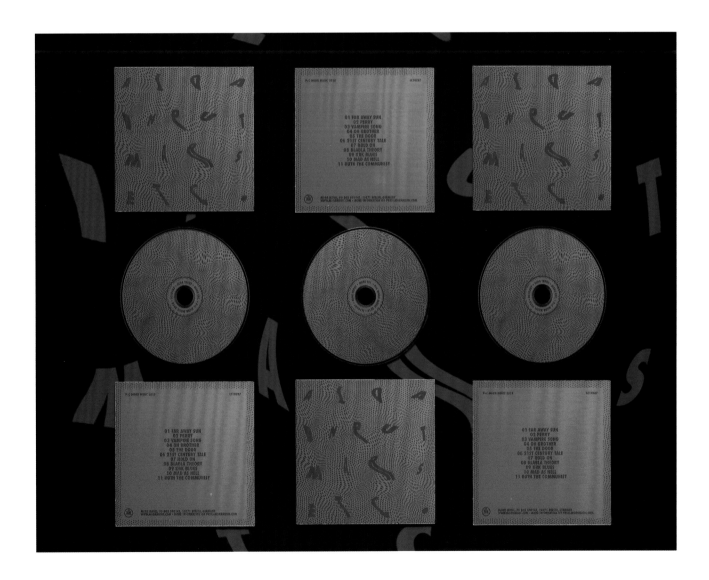

Art Direction, Creative Direction & Design:
— **Thomas Neulinger**

Client:
— **Necro Deathmort**

— EP3

With *EP3* Necro Deathmort were once more expanding their unique blend of electronic music. Thomas created a range of bright high contrast gradients and textures through an array of distortion and refraction. Then he used them as components for an abstract digital collage in his interpretation of the song "Holy Prism," to depict the sun god giving birth to the sun.

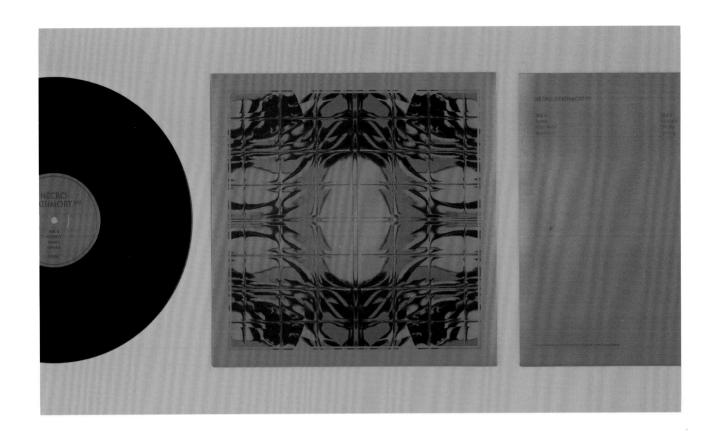

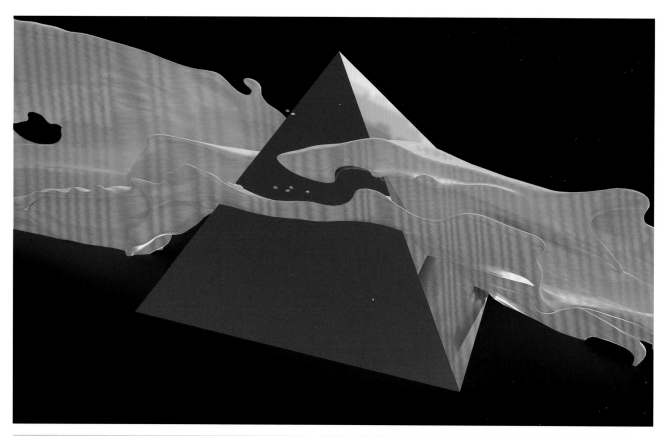

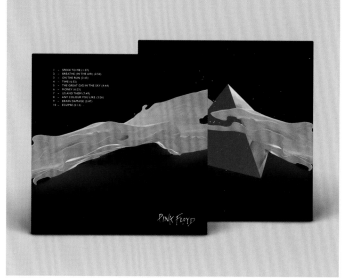

Pink Floyd
—— Album Cover

Andonni created this fan-made album cover design based on the album *The Dark Side of the Moon* by Pink Floyd. The refraction of the light producing the different colours from the original album is something that Andonni wanted to exaggerate in his version. He was aiming for a more psychedelic feel which he especially experienced in the songs "Brain Damage" and "Any Colour You Like."

Design:
— **Andonni Tsolingkas**

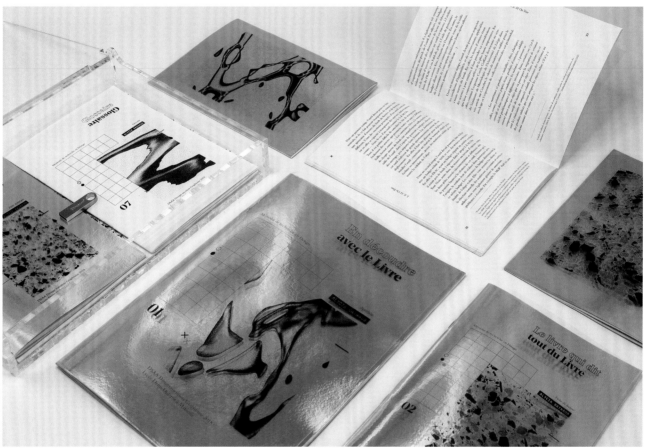

En découdre
avec le Livre

This project is a master's graphic design thesis of Alycia in 2018. She explored what codex is as a symbol, an ordinal form, and an open form in her thesis. She used a transparent and holographic 3D layer as the cover to embody a book's hybrid nature. She also crystallised how order and disorder can be parts of a book's shape while referencing it to the human psyche.

Design:
— **Alycia Rainaud**

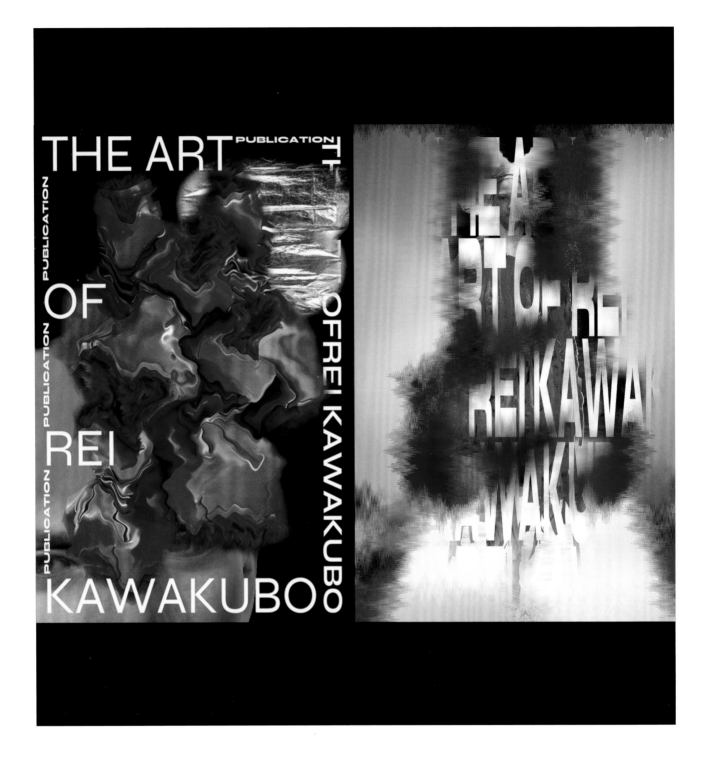

The Art of Rei Kawakubo

This editorial project is a tribute to the great Japanese designer Rei Kawakubo whose incredible creations represent the expression of an authentic pioneer of style. Brando wants to share his opinion: What I do is not influenced by what happens in the world of fashion or culture, I start with abstract images to create a new concept of beauty.

Design:
— **Brando Corradini**

Nefes

The inspiration for Mercan Dede's album cover project is Ebru art. Fatih tried to combine the abstract word "nefes (breath)" with Ebru art. Such an image has become a fusion of digital and traditional techniques.

Design & Photography:
— **Fatih Hardal**

Client:
— **Mercan Dede**

Burn Again

Burn Again is the debut EP of electro-rock band Playful Spark. Max tried to mix black and bright colour on the cover. Also, Max added some elements of unusual fire on the cover to associate with the unusual sounds in some songs from this album.

Art Direction & Design:
— **Max Genesiis**

Client:
— **Playful Spark**

Photography:
— **Josch13**

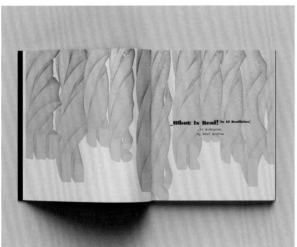

Hyperirrealism

This project's graphic design is a visual statement that intends to create a particular environment that fluctuates between multiple dimensional planes through the use of 2D and 3D typography, 2D as a representation of reality and 3D as a recreation of a virtual, multidimensional, and fractal space in people's imagination. The pastel colour helps complement an ethereal and provocative atmosphere.

Graphic Design:
— **Diego Pinilla Amaya**

Client:
— **Ale Girá**

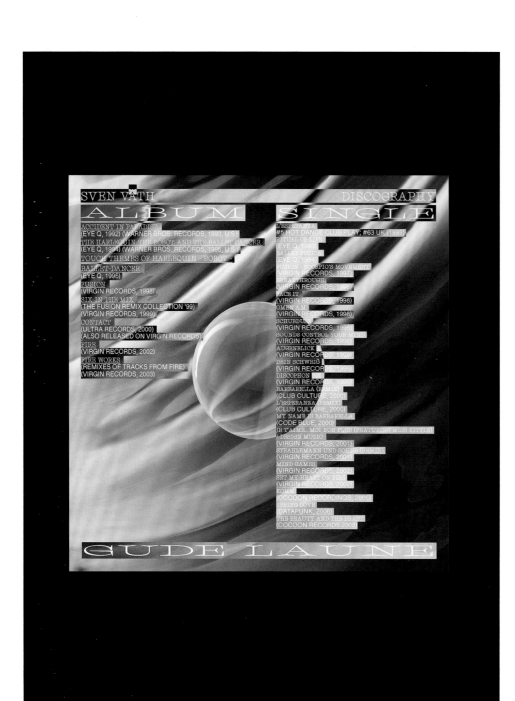

Design:
— Brando Corradini

Sven Väth
Greatest Hits 1982-2017

It is a project coming from Brando's passion for techno music. Sven Väth's techno music led him to study as a DJ. And Sven Väth is one of the greatest exponents of electronic music worldwide. In this project, Brando elaborated the packaging of the album of Sven Väth's major record works.

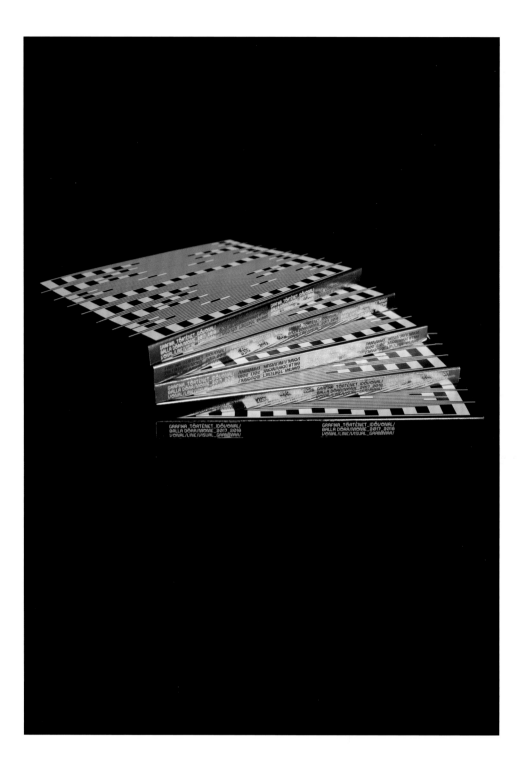

Graphic Design & Photography:
— **Dora Balla**

Client & Publishing:
— **Moholy-Nagy University
of Art and Design (MOME)**

Graphic Design
—— **Timeline I Line**

"A line is a dot that went for a walk." This quote from Paul Klee tells people a lot. The historical timeline and the infinite line in fine art both symbolise the timelessness and the process itself. This book project consists of the project of curriculum development and the annual work of the visual grammar course at Moholy-Nagy University of Art and Design. And this is the first Hungarian publication about the 100-year historical timeline of contemporary graphic design.

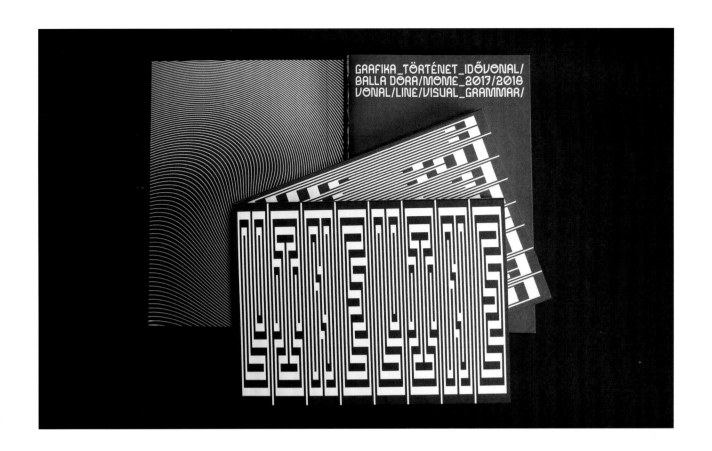

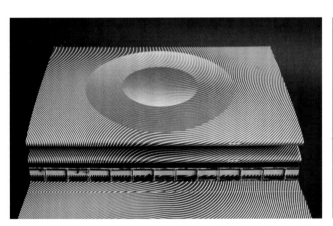

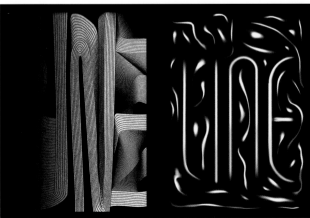

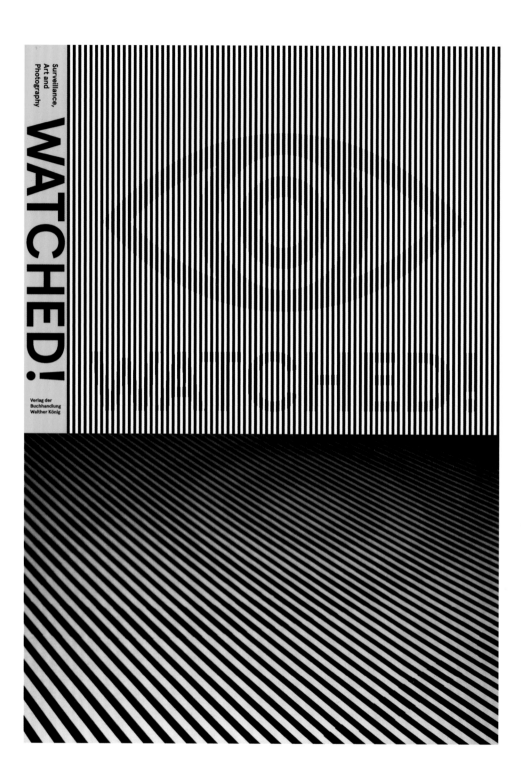

Design Agency:
— **BankerWessel**

Client:
— **Hasselblad Foundation**

— WATCHED!

BankerWessel designed the book and invitation with an optical illusion for the exhibition *WATCHED! Surveillance, Art, and Photography*. This book with 300 pages is an extensive compendium of the works of many artists and photographers reflecting upon the impacts of surveillance.

Design & Photography:
— **Dora Balla**

Client:
— **Moholy-Nagy University
of Art and Design (MOME)**

— Visual Grammar No.I

This book is a summary and educational resource for the course of MOME Visual Grammar. The theme is related to the form of the circle, Max Bill's works, and Zero Group's works and philosophy. This book was printed with 4+1 Pantone colours and was published with four different cover designs.

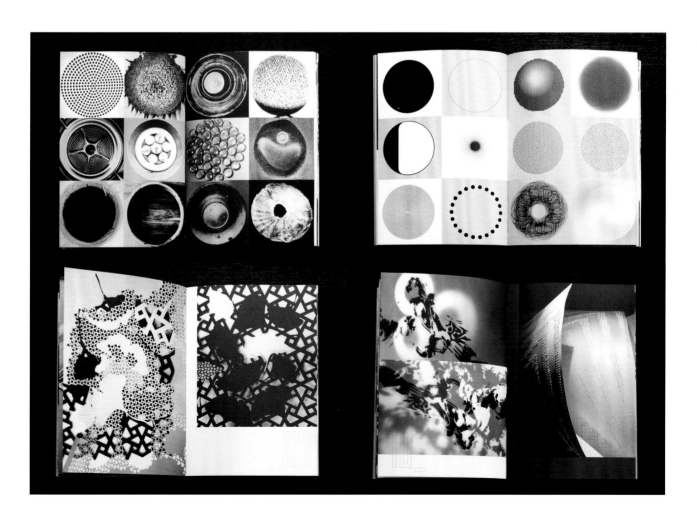

Blurryface

Blurryface is the fourth album of Twenty One Pilots. This project was an assignment of Guadalupe's typography class. The aim was to design a cover artwork in which typography played the main role. And distortion is the main focus of this artwork. The zigzag effect was achieved by repeatedly printing and moving the typography when scanning it. Later, Guadalupe enhanced some part of this artwork by software.

Design:
— **Guadalupe Peyrallo**

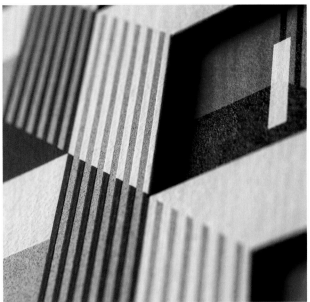

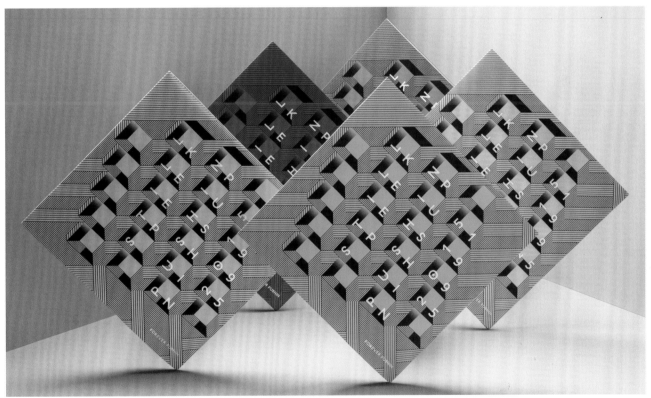

Keep Pushin'

The design of Boris Dlugosch's anniversary album shows pureness, sense of geometry, with a little complexity and playfulness. Detroit's concrete, urban straightforwardness, and vibrant colours serve as the design ingredients. And the font GT Haptik provides necessary rectilinearity with a playful twist.

Design Agency:
— **Paperlux Studio**

Creative Direction:
— **Max Kuehne**

Art Direction:
— **Lisa Keiffer**

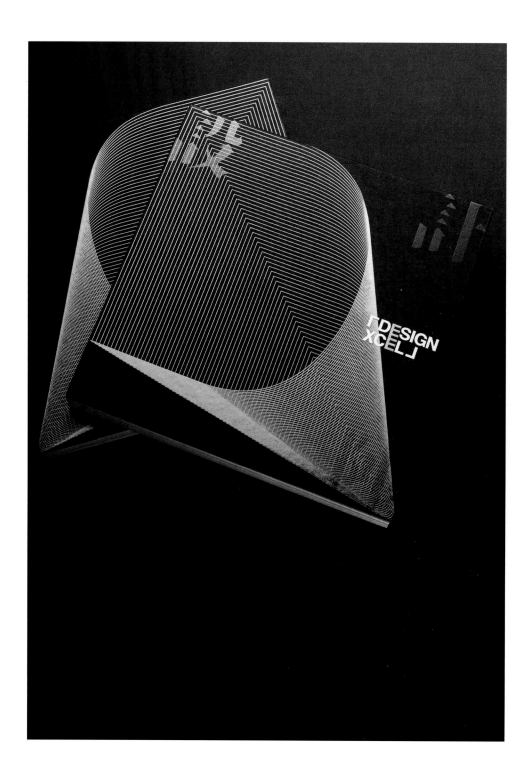

DesignXcel

As the first-ever joint-school design exhibition in Hong Kong, China, DesignXcel was held by DCHK. This book project was designed by FUNDAMENTAL. Two fluorescent spot colours were used to shape the book's overall sense during the printing. Meanwhile, the cover and back cover were stamped with green and blue colour.

Design Agency:
— **FUNDAMENTAL**

Client:
— **Design Council of Hong Kong (DCHK)**

Creciente

Creciente is the first solo album of the Peruvian rock artist Toño Jauregui.
Paloma created a geometric structure made out of the 3D letters stacked on top
of each other spelling the album title. The contrast between the dark blue and
bright gradient that emerges through many windows and doors of the structure
creates an illusion of the existence of a brighter world.

Design:
— **Paloma Pizarro**

Client:
— **Toño Jauregui**

Black Sands

This project is a reinterpretation and redesign of the album *Black Sands* by English DJ Bonobo.

Design:
— **Sofía Mele**

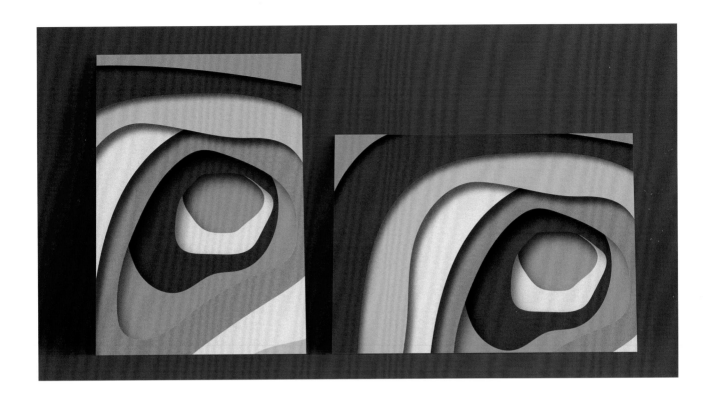

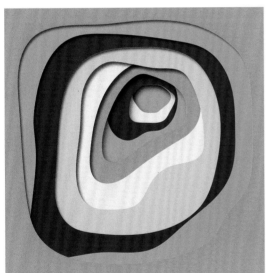

Vinyl Project

Anna got inspired by tunnel books during the project's creation. Anna thought
that applying a shadow into a composition is always a good way to create the
illusion of distance between objects. Five different colours and sheets' shadow
altogether created this cover with a distinct illusion of a papercut tunnel.

Design:
— **Anna Gruszkowska**

Design:
— **Mathieu Delestre**

BuröNeko Graphic
Notebook 2017

For the foundation of his graphic design studio BuröNeko, Mathieu decided to create an original graphic notebook printed by risograph with illustrations and patterns in fluo colour. Mathieu considers it as a graphic playground for visual experimentation using limited colours and texture of risography.

Art & Concept Direction:
— **Cesar Martinez**

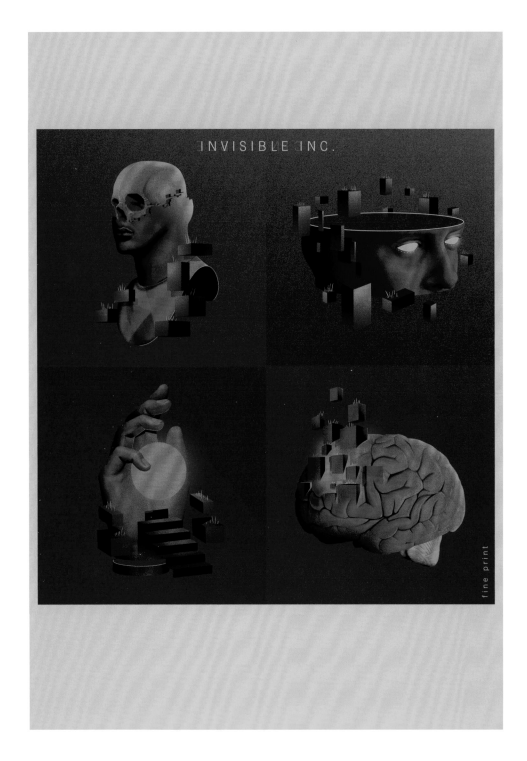

___ Invisible Inc. _____

Cesar's goal was to create the concept, logo, and design for Invisible Inc.'s second album *Fine Print*. The illustrations represent every member's contribution to the band's concept and music—one of them provides the vision of the sounds, another is the heart of the lyrics. The brain represents the effervescent intelligence while the hand is the pillar that unifies all the elements.

fine print

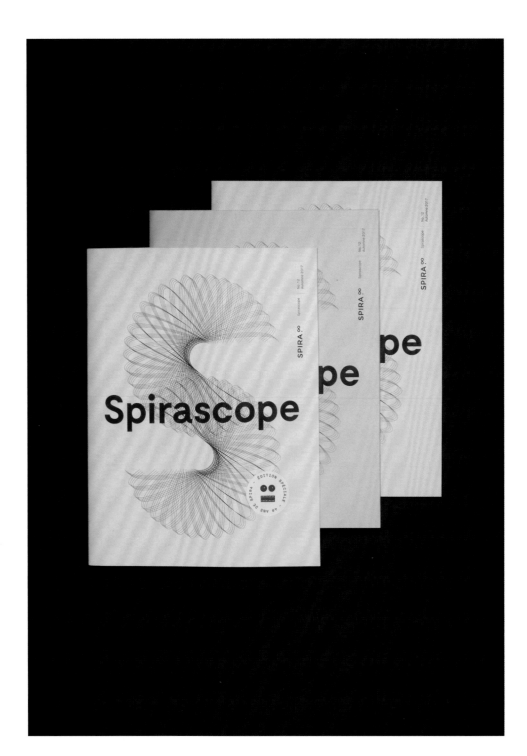

Design Agency:
— **Figure**

*Design, Art Direction,
Creative Direction &
Illustration:*
— **Jeremy Hall**

Client:
— **Spira**

Spirascope

Figure was commissioned to make a special edition of the *Spirascope*—a printed newspaper which was published by Spira in the 90s. Forty years later, Spira had the idea to revive this document to reveal the known and unknown parts of its history and to illustrate its evolution. Figure was to design this newspaper as a trip in the 90s. Like the cover made with the Spirograph, all the elements were designed to reflect the nostalgia.

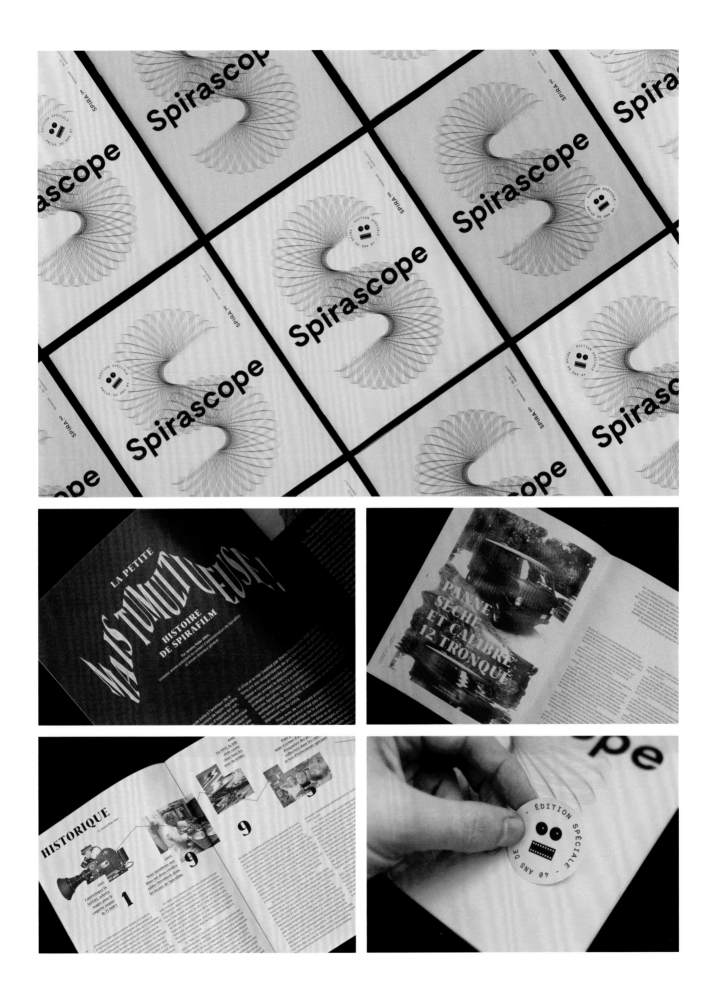

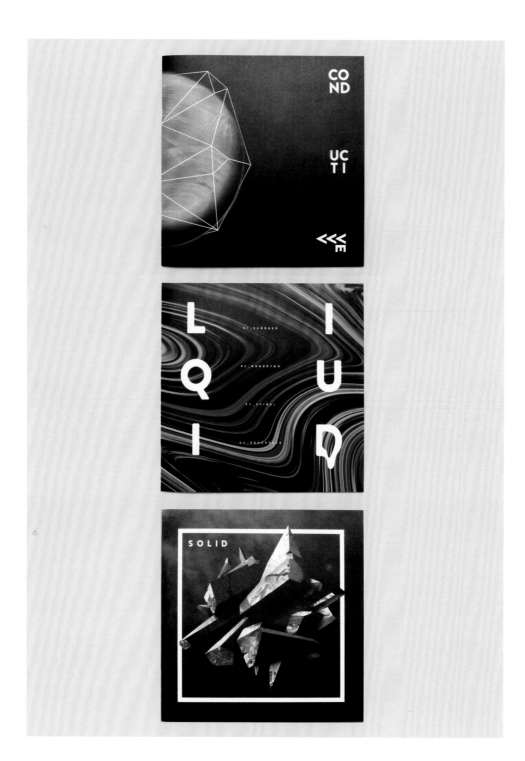

Design Agency:
— Forth + Back

Client:
— Alex Miklovic

Audio Visual

Audio Visual is an album series exploring the method of designing an album's packaging in unison with the creation of its music. The designers decided on trying to translate different properties or states of metal into an audio-visual journey of sorts. What came about were three albums—*Solid*, *Liquid*, and *Conductive*—where in which both parties would sample sounds and visuals that related to those three chosen themes.

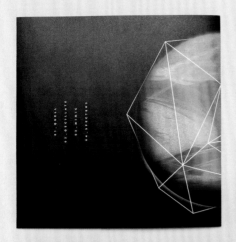
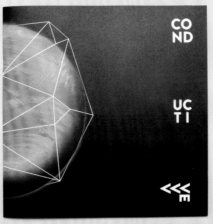

Design Agency:
— **AKU**

__ PART

This book was published in conjunction with the Young Architect's Prize. Instead of renders, photographed models are used to depict the work. They are placed on a grid, giving a sense of space and scale. An experimental headline typeface connects the grid and the architects' modular objects. People can design their own cover by placing the object stickers in the imaginary space.

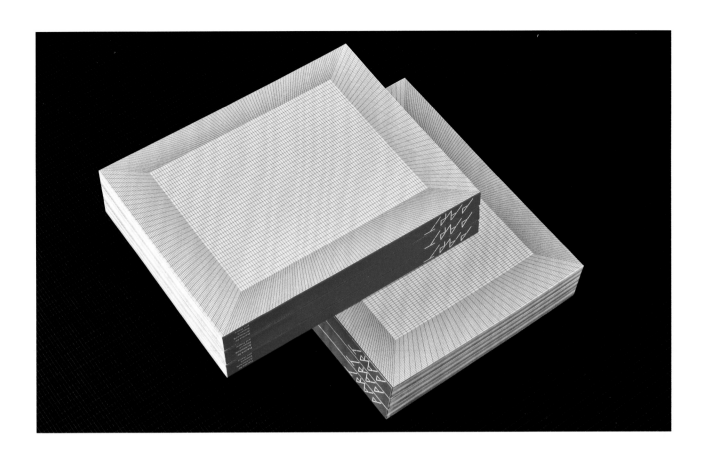

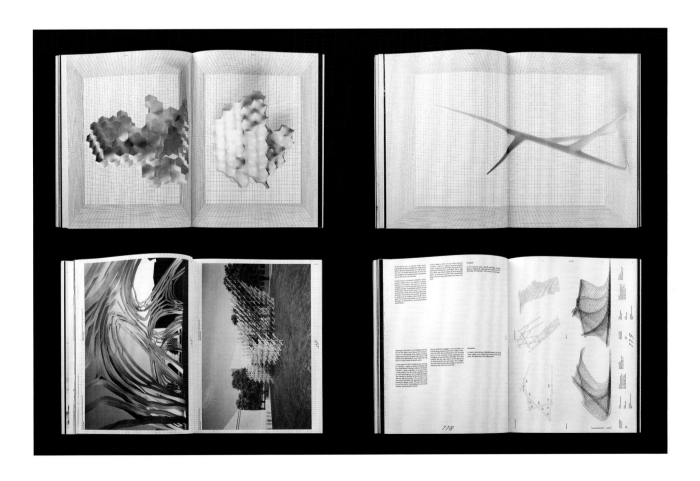

Design:
— **Vicente García Morillo**

Creative Direction:
— **Michele Salati**

Client:
— **UNICEF**

Photography:
— **Robert G. Bartholot**

— UNICEF ECHO

Vicente was commissioned by J. Walter Thompson Zurich to create a campaign for UNICEF focused on the issue of 100 million girls vanishing worldwide. The challenging concept was focusing on creating awareness of these horrible crimes. And Vicente's responsibility for this project included creating the cover design and typography treatment for the ECHO campaign.

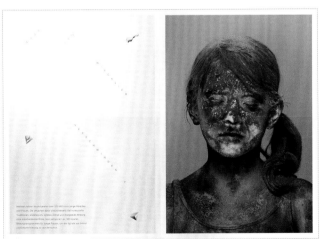

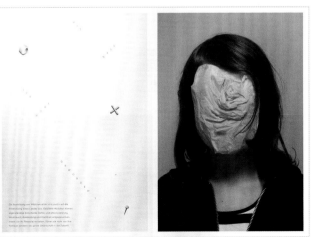

Design Agency:
— **JOEFANGSTUDIO**

Graphic Design:
— **Joe Fang**
— **FKWU**
— **Hitsu Pi**

Client:
— **Feeling Good Music Co.**

As Good
— As Water

In order to echo the free-flowing experimental jazz music of Minyen Hsieh, JOEFANGSTUDIO used oil-water separation characteristics to film altered letterings through a glass, then processed them into layers of spot varnish, PVC printing, and skeletal CD printing in graphics software. The multiple layers of filming, ripple-like layout design, and diverse transparent textures and printing were all used to demonstrate the pureness and liquidity of water.

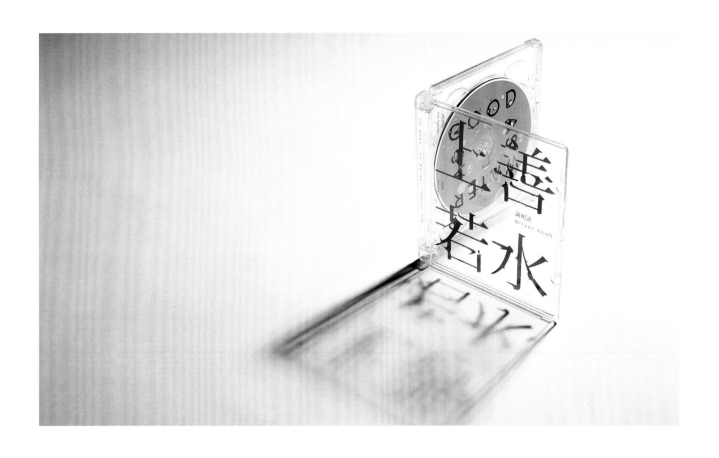

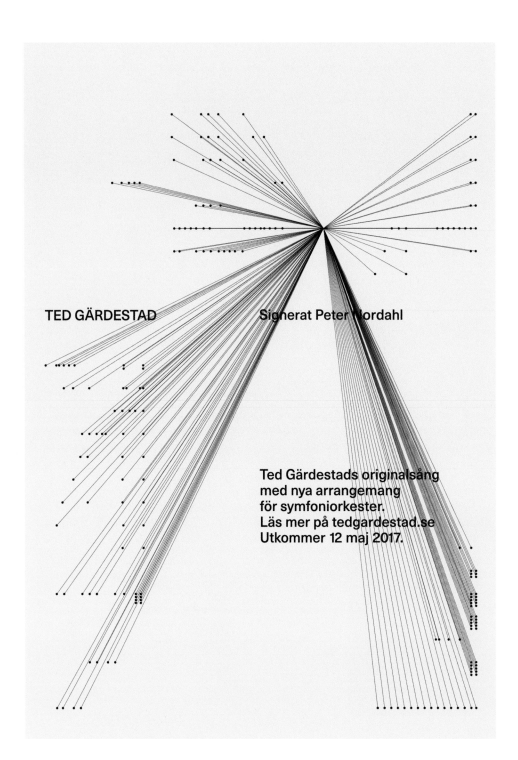

TED GÄRDESTAD

Signerat Peter Nordahl

Ted Gärdestads originalsång
med nya arrangemang
för symfoniorkester.
Läs mer på tedgardestad.se
Utkommer 12 maj 2017.

Design Agency:
— **Stockholm
Design Lab (SDL)**

Design:
— **István Vasil**
— **Lukas Nässil**

Client:
— **Universal Music (Sweden)**

Client Direction:
— **Anneli Myrin Holloway**

The Remastering
of Ted Gärdestad

SDL was asked to visualise the remastering of Ted Gärdestad, one of
Sweden's most acclaimed and beloved recording artists. The identity
system is highly recognisable yet flexible, where each song has its unique
composition based on the notes. Black is used as background for singles
and white for the album. In the motion, the elements embody scenes drawn
from the lyrics that flow with the music and follow its dynamics.

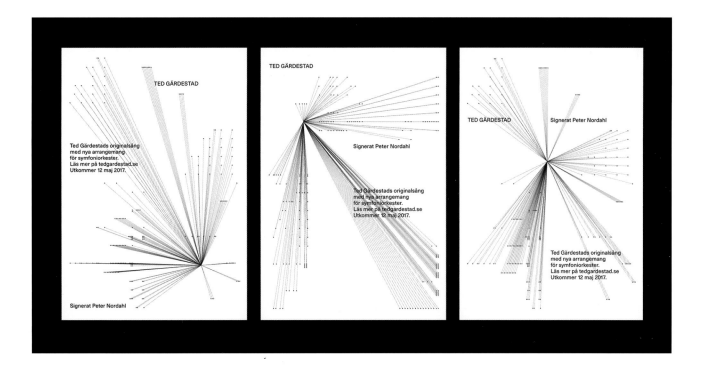

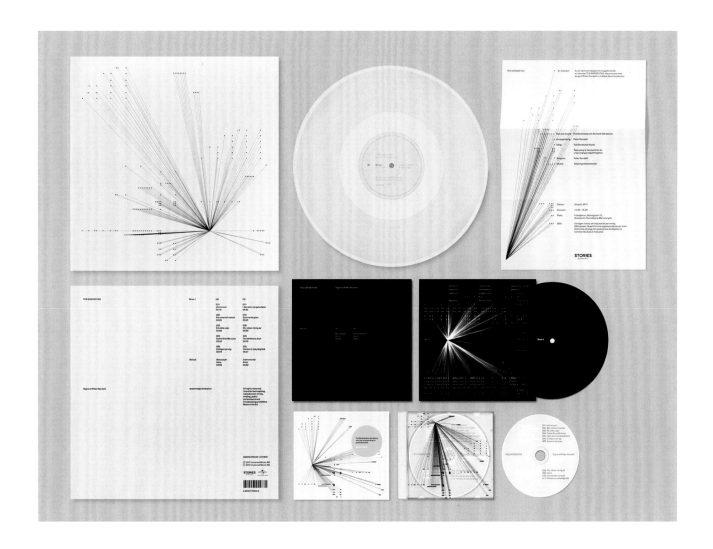

Design:
— **Karolína Pálková**

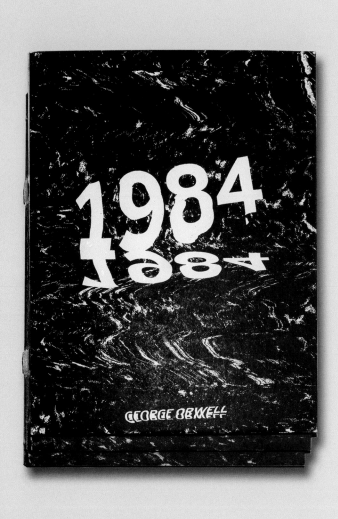

George Orwell 1984

This project divides *1984* into three main parts where the story gradually escalates. Karolína decided to make an open binding, which shapes a nice look. Also, there are illustrations inside the book, which describe Karolína's view of *1984*.

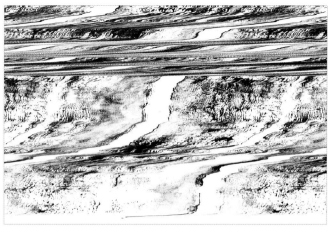

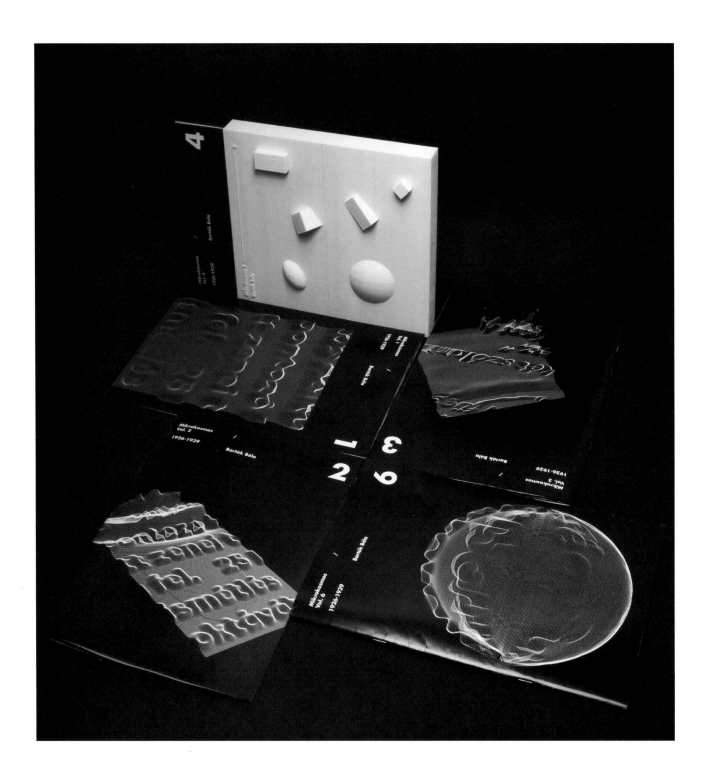

Mikrokosmos

Mikrokosmos is a special edition monograph consisting of 153 progressive piano pieces by Béla Bartók, presented in a minimalist 3D-printed case. Each cover was assigned a geometric figure built up in a point-grid system referring to the structure of the cosmos. The grid points were then animated to the rhythm of the given piece, gradually forming the typography of its title in a spatial form on the white cover.

Design:
— **Nóra Kaszanyi**

Supervision:
— **Dora Balla**

Photography:
— **Sarah Szatmári**

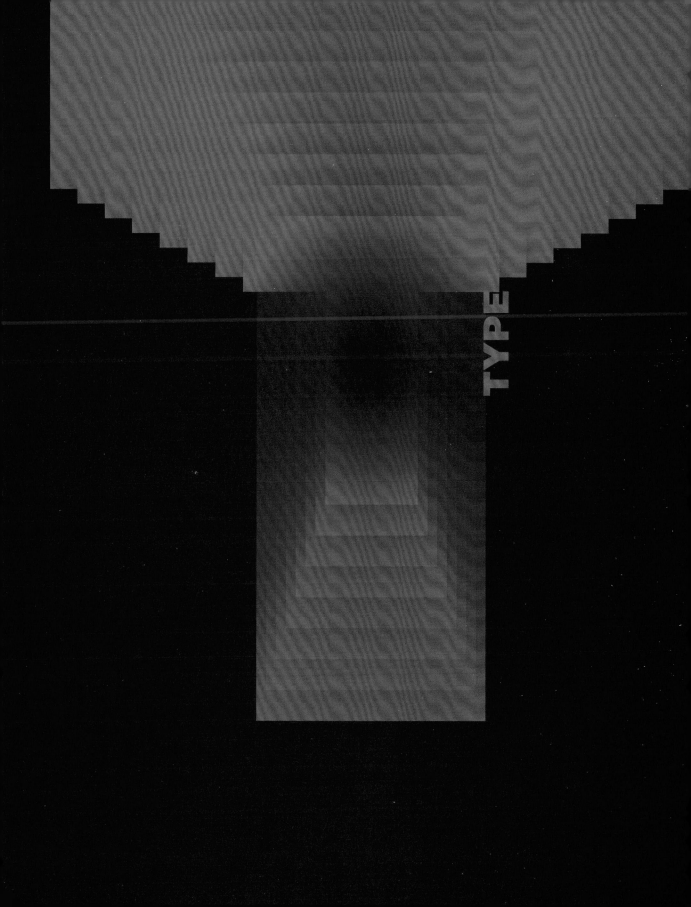

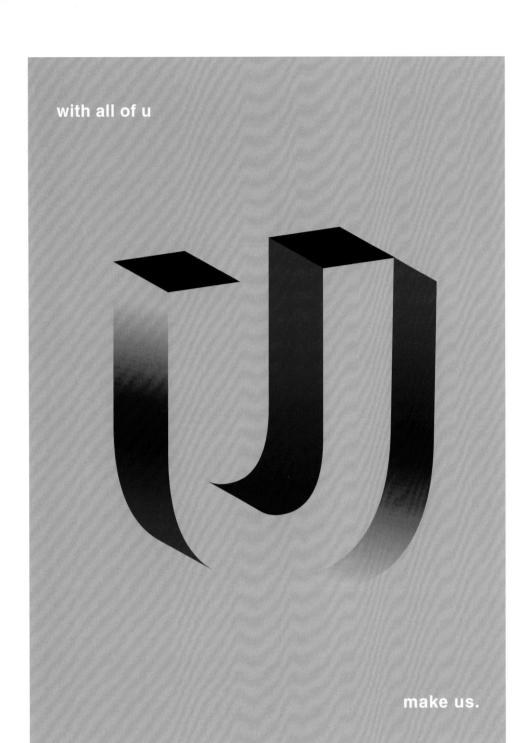

Design
— **Kevin Lam**

with all of u

make us.

___ **All of U** _____

Kevin tried to describe his perspective on the word "US" through this project. He broke apart the "US" and understood that "US" does not necessarily mean two persons physically being together. "US" could be any state of a relationship, hence Kevin transformed the letter "U" in different shapes to express this idea behind it.

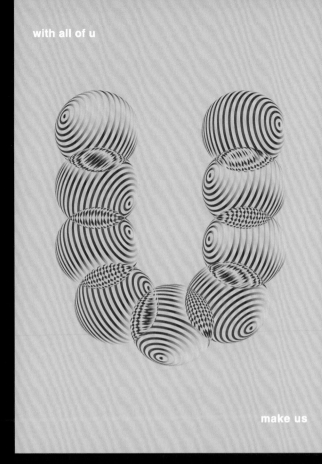

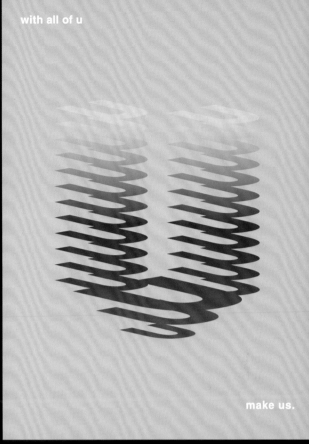

make us

make us.

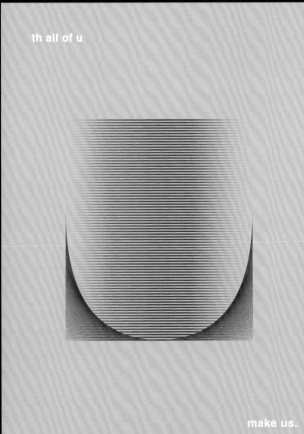

make us.

make us.

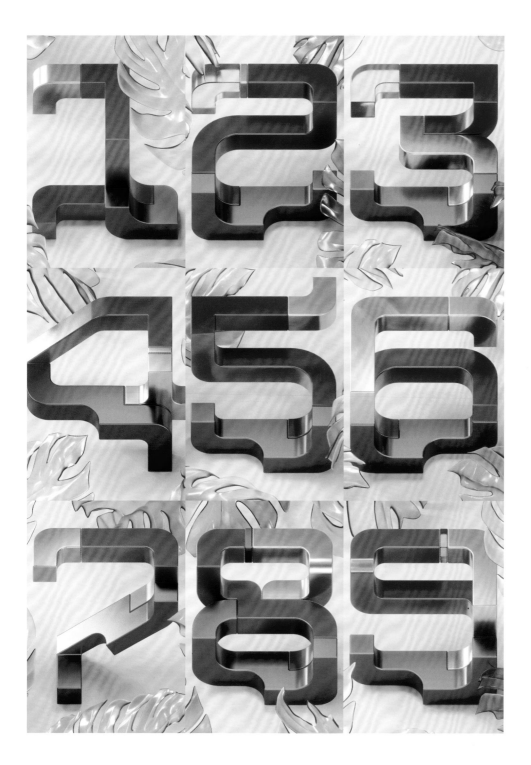

Art & Creative Direction:
— **BÜRO UFHO**

— **36 Days of Type** ——————

BÜRO UFHO explored the idea of 3D typography being much more than just adding depth to a 2D typeface. Many of BÜRO UFHO's sculptural explorations play with the perspective illusion, where the letters can only be seen from a certain angle, and the results are a fine tension between the abstract forms and legibility function of letters.

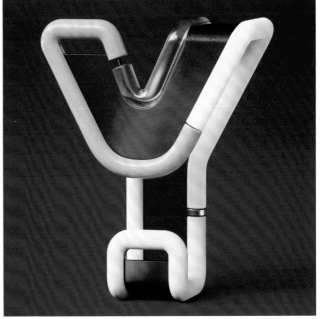

Imperfecta

This sculptural numeral system exploration inspired by imperfecta, a disorder characterised by bones that break easily. Each number is broken down into smaller individual parts, shifted slightly away from each other that create grooves and edges, resulting in an imperfect form.

Art & Creative Direction:
— **BÜRO UFHO**

ABCDEFGHIJ
KLMNOPQRS
TUVWXYZ

Shadow Font

Shadow Font was created for the single *You Got Me Under Control* by Dr!ve &
Bowser. The font is based on Kai Matthiesen's self-created grotesque that was
created at the Royal College of Art in London. The aim was to create a version of
a grotesque font that is sort of stencilled and with a 3D illusion.

Design:
— **Kai Damian Matthiesen**

IGGY POP

Design:
— **José Bernabé**

___ Life Tracks ___

José's goal for this project was to tribute to his favourite songs accompanying along his life. The effect was mainly made by customised brushes, the mixer brush, and Photoshop's Liquify tool. The most important part was to make an interesting composition and use a proper attractive combination of colours. José utilised the lights and shadows to overlap the letters and achieved 3D effects.

Bomb the Bass

David Bowie

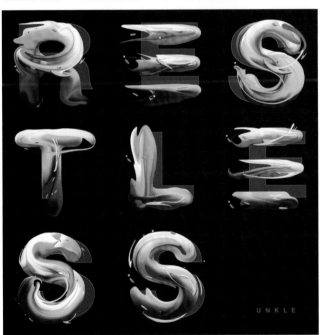

UNKLE

Iggy Pop

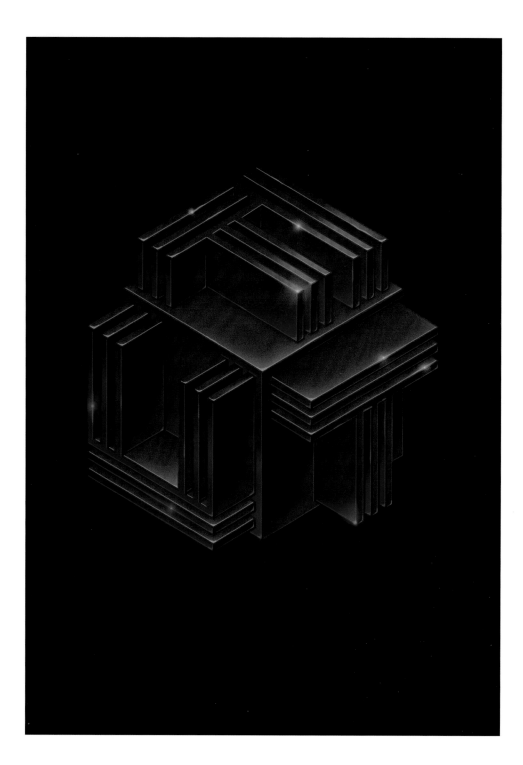

Design:
— **Joan Ramon Pastor (Wete)**

Typography
— Experiments —————————————

As a graphic designer who makes letterings and fonts, Joan is always open to using different resources or mixing disciplines. In this project, he wanted to design a series of typographical experiments to practice some 3D techniques.

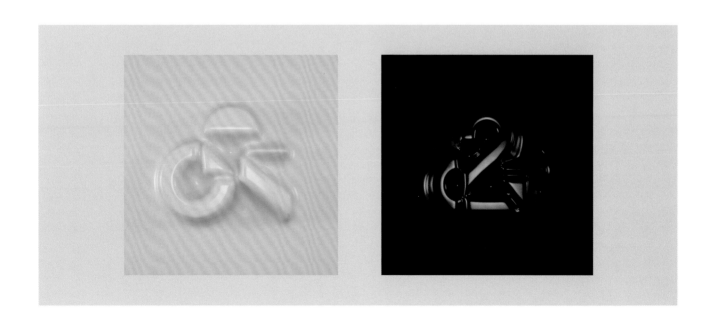

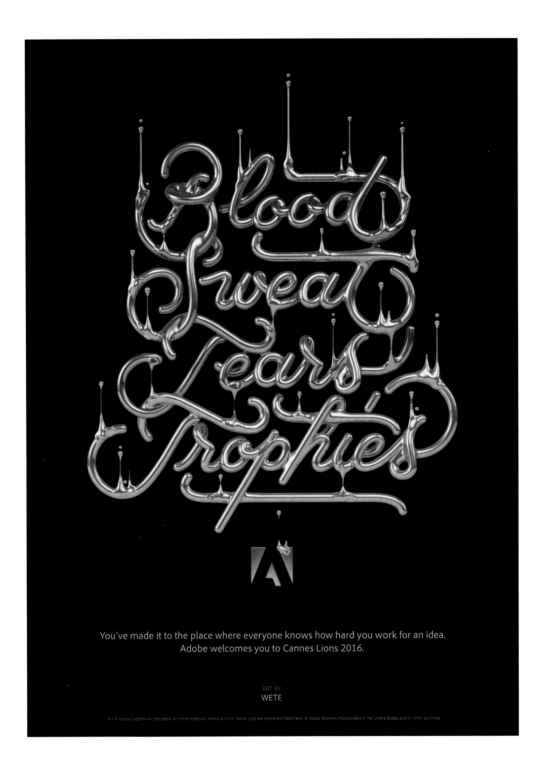

Adobe: Blood
Sweat Tears Campaign

Adobe developed a campaign with a concept that let the participants of Cannes Lions Festival know how truly hard they were nominated. Joan took the familiar expression "blood, sweat, and tears" and gave it an unexpected twist with "trophies." And these words were executed in a series of stunning typographic processing from different typographers.

Design:
— **Joan Ramon Pastor (Wete)**

Creative Direction:
— **Kashka Pregowska-Czerw**

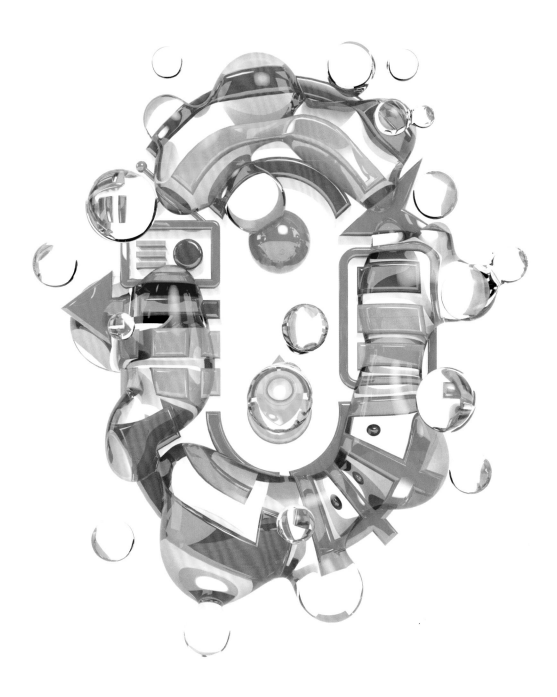

SEAT: Start Moving

Letter "O" was designed for the SEAT campaign "Start Moving" with the Spanish magazine *Yorokobu*. For this campaign, they chose eleven designers including Joan who had to represent one letter each. The main idea was to represent the car's movement and connectivity.

Design:
— **Joan Ramon Pastor (Wete)**

Design:
— **Joan Ramon Pastor (Wete)**

3D Assistance:
— **Eric Genesis**

Yorokobu

This is a typographic project for the calendar of Spanish magazine *Yorokobu*. The idea was to create a calendar with some creative advice. For this purpose, Joan designed a series of 3D letterings (one per month) that attempt to represent in a subjective manner.

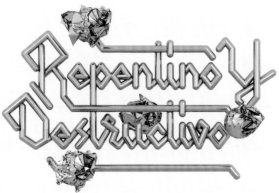

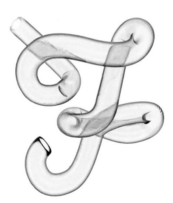

Design:
— **Aaron Kaufman**

Glass Type

This project is an experimentation with glass forms using a combination of digital and 2D techniques. This bright and modern typography collection has unique and improbable shapes that question the relationship among form, reality, and materiality.

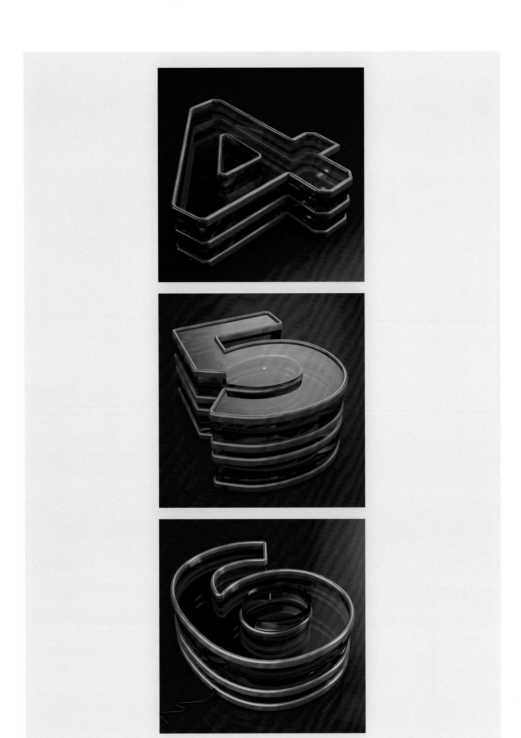

Design:
— **Muhammad
Ridzwan Sakamat**

36 Days of Type

In this project, Ridzwan Sakamat created a font that must come up with a highly original design. He experimented with colours and basic shapes in the typography design.

Design:
— **eltipo**

— **36 Days of Type**

For the contribution of the 2017 project 36 Days of Type, eltipo was experimenting in Adobe Illustrator with different styles and effects that create a certain depth of 3D effect. This project was later transformed into a wooden artwork which was exhibited at the "Don't Believe The Type" Expo in 2017.

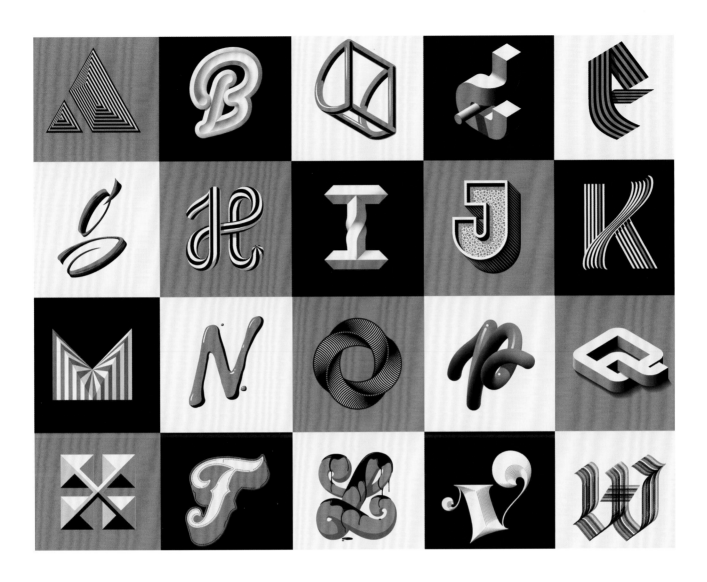

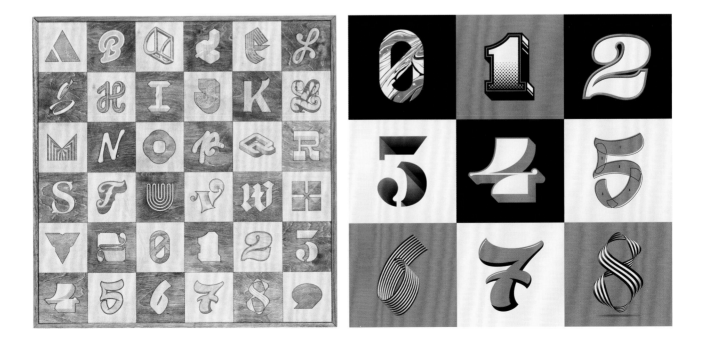

Control

Sergey regards this project as explorations in distorted typography, performed for various films, music, and graphic design. Sergey got inspired by the chaotic scenes in Berlin's clubs. In this project words and phrases are not stable anymore, being deconstructed and morphed into glitch and noise.

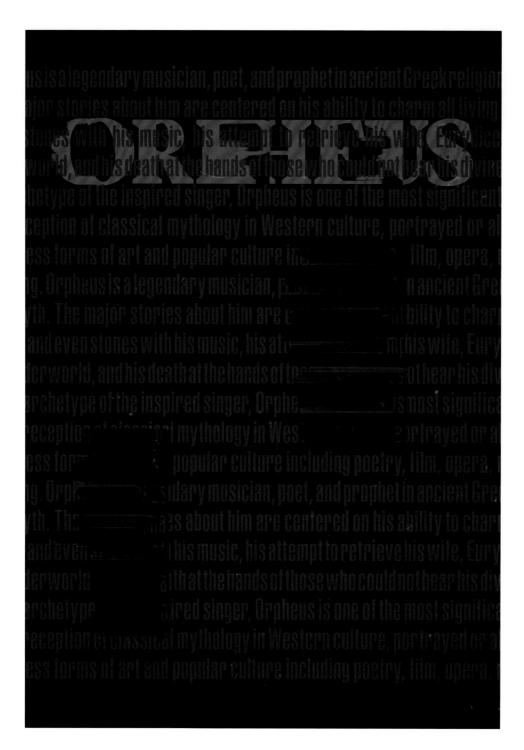

Design:
— **Sergey Skip**

___ Orpheus

This project is the artwork for EP *Orpheus* of the electronic music artist and producer Tim Aminov. Explorations are based on the mythological background of the death of Orpheus, the ancient Greek musician and poet who was ripped into shreds by Maenads. Sergey tried to abstract and visualise such an idea to a single word.

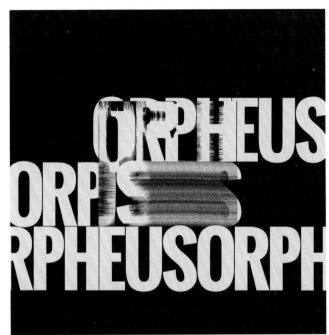
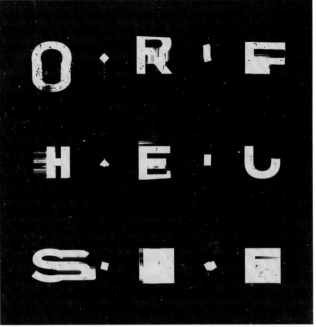

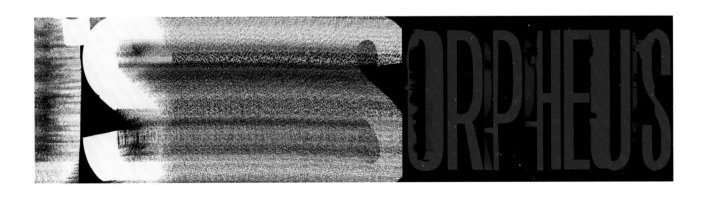

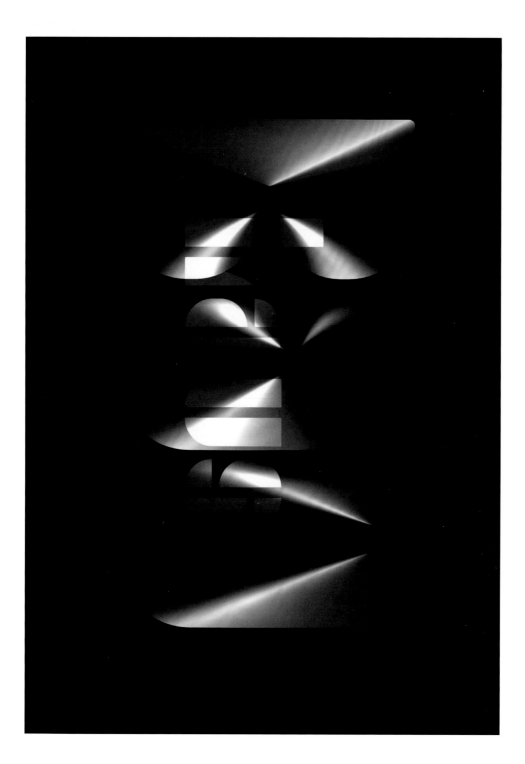

Design:
— **Andrew Footit**

Adobe Hidden Treasures
- Bauhaus Dessau

This project is Andrew's contribution to the #adobehidden-treasures story. Andrew wanted to show off some letters of font Joschmi in his own way. This idea was to bring the history almost lost from the Bauhaus Dessau into the modern day.

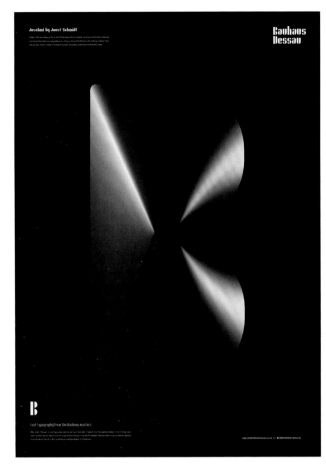

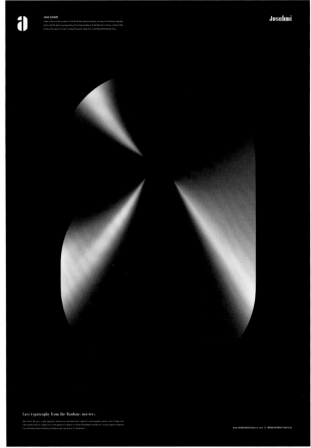

Design:
— **Andrés E. Ávila B.**

___ **Third Time Lucky** _____

This project was Andrés' third consecutive participation in the challenge "36 Days of Type." This project was inspired by classic logos. Andrés created volumetric shapes with optical effects, different patterns, lines in sequence, and impossible figures.

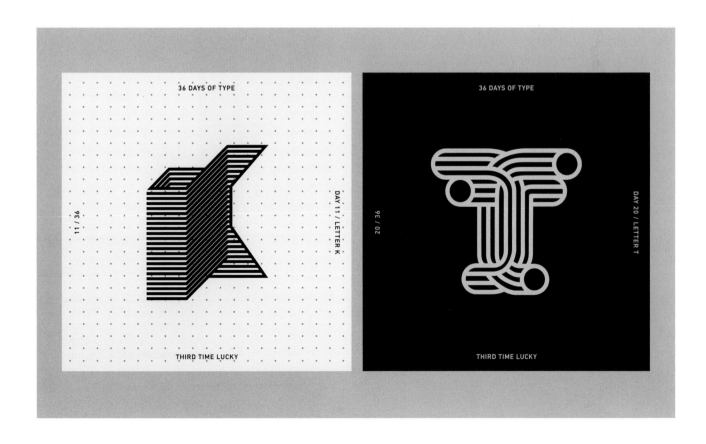

Design:
— **Txaber Mentxaka**

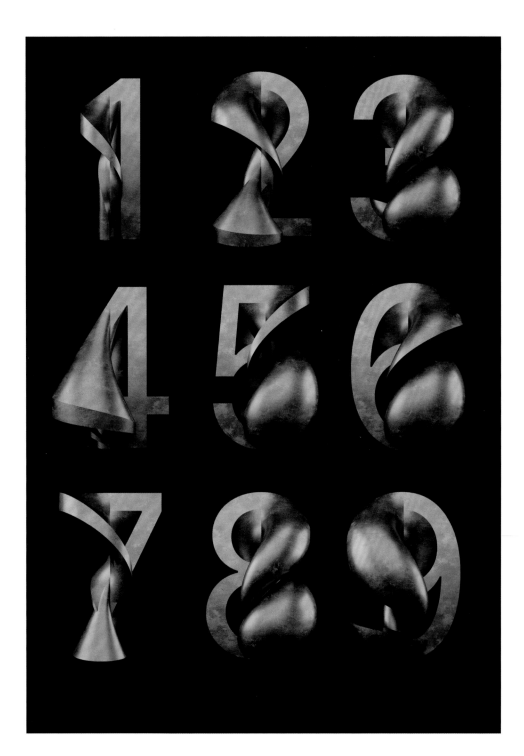

Rotation Typography

This project is an experimental typeface based on the partial rotation of the geometry. The aesthetic result with the metallic texture shows a recognisable character with great sculptural strength.

Design:
— **Txaber Mentxaka**

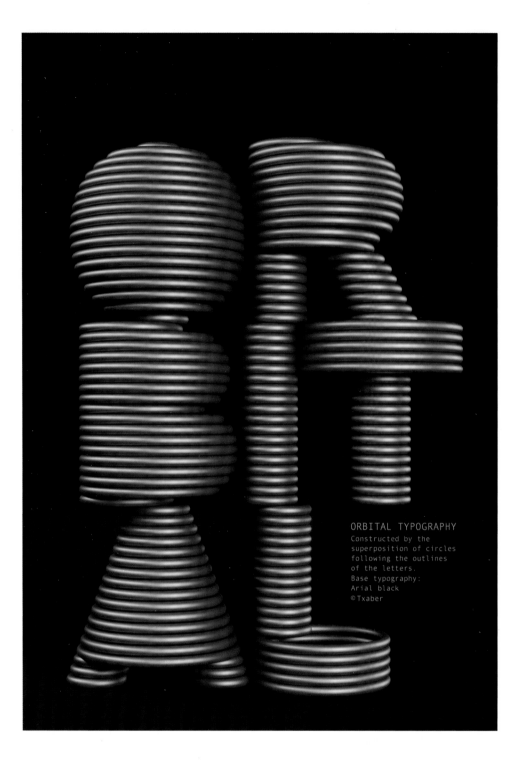

ORBITAL TYPOGRAPHY
Constructed by the
superposition of circles
following the outlines
of the letters.
Base typography:
Arial black
©Txaber

Orbital Typography

Txaber used Arial Black as the basic typography to create this experimental project. The orbital typography is constructed by superposition of circles following the outlines of the letters.

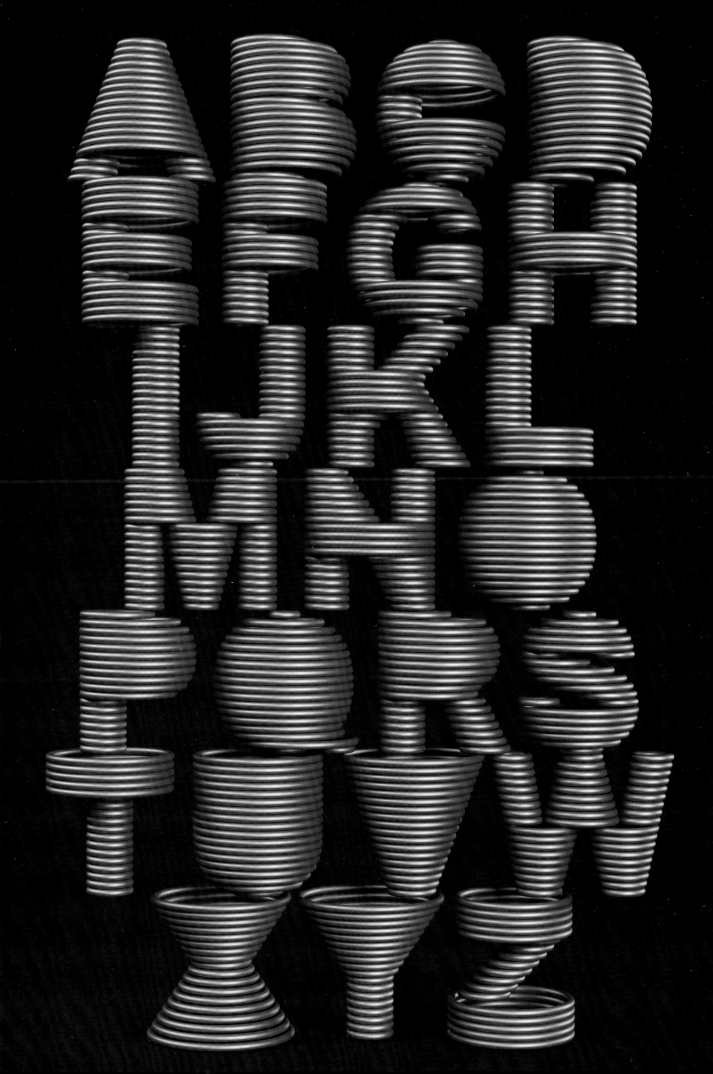

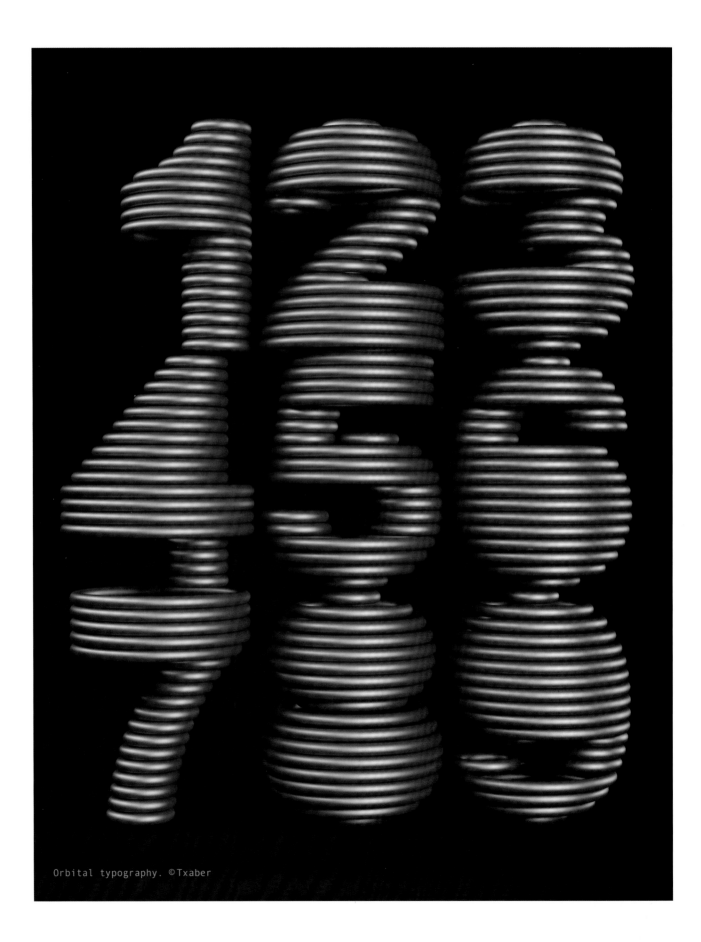

Orbital typography. ©Txaber

INDEX

Anton Synytsia

behance.net/leggo

Anton Synytsia is an art director based in Ternopil, Ukraine. He is specialising in branding and poster design.

P152–153

Atelier Baudelaire, GeneralPublic

atelierbaudelaire.com
generalpublic.fr

Atelier Baudelaire and GeneralPublic are two Paris-based design studios specialising in the field of culture. They both work separately and sometimes gather forces to collaborate on demanding projects such as visual identities, publishing, signage, posters, and communication design.

P038–039, P096–097

Atelier Irradié

Irradie.com

Atelier Irradié is a multidisciplinary creative studio founded in 2016 by brothers Alain and Laurent Vonck. They bring visual and conceptual solutions in the fields of graphic design, art direction, and digital design. Their skill expresses branding, graphical systems, publications, and digital interfaces for a variety of clients.

P034–035, P078–079, P136–137

Atelier Minuit

atelierminuit.com

Atelier Minuit is a French creative studio founded by Anthéa Ferreira and Benoit Hody in Paris.

P154

BankerWessel

bankerwessel.com

BankerWessel is an award-winning studio with extensive experience in the field of visual identities, exhibition design, publications, and digital media. They are the first and foremost a team of devoted graphic designers wanting to create visually strong, original and memorable solutions for all kinds of media.

P170–171

Brando Corradini

brandocorradinigrafik.info

Brando Corradini is a Roman graphic designer who is passionate about graphics, architecture, fashion, design, and music, which accompany him throughout the day becoming an important source of inspiration from which to draw.

P162, P166–167

BRID

brid.me

BRID is a unique brand identity of Ia Darakhvelidze, a graphic designer from Tbilisi, Georgia. BRID is working on brands, books, logos, prints, web pages, packaging, illustrations, and so on. BRID helps its clients create brands with compelling visual identities that will make an impact in clients' industries and build a long-lasting relationship between brand and community.

P116–119

Bunch

bunchdesign.com

Bunch is a design studio offering a diverse range of work including identity, literature, art direction, digital, and motion. Established in 2005 with an international reach, from London to Zagreb, Bunch delivers intelligent and innovative cross-platform solutions of communication design.

P072–073

BÜRO UFHO

ufho.com

BÜRO UFHO is a multi-disciplinary creative studio based in Singapore delivering beautifully crafted solutions for aspiring clients around the world.

P202–203, P204

Caterina Bianchini Studio

caterinabianchini.com

Caterina Bianchini Studio is an independent and multi-award winning studio in London. The studio's ethos is firmly grounded in art, conceptual ideas, and experimentation. Each project challenges current design norms by creating unique typographic layouts and carefully curated colour palettes.

P106–109

Cesar Martinez

theblackdynasty.com

Cesar Martinez is an illustrator and art director from Mexico City. After working in the advertisement industry for a number of years, he founded an animation studio and brought in a wide range of clients ranging from Nike and Mazda to liquor brands such as Jose Cuervo and Smirnoff.

P182–183

Chia Hao Hsu

behance.net/xudesignco

Chia Hao Hsu is a visual designer based in Taipei, China.

P068–069

Classmate Studio

classmatestudio.com

Classmate Studio is a design team based in Hungary and Finland. Their main fields are in brand identities and editorial design, influenced by modern graphic design principles.

P042–043

Clémence Gouy

behance.net/clemencegouy

Clémence Gouy is a graphic designer and illustrator graduated from the École de Communication Visuelle of Nantes, France.

P110–111

Daó, Pedro Veneziano

estudiodao.com
pedroveneziano.com

Daó is a Brazilian studio formed by Giovani Castelucci, Guilherme Vieira, and Giulia Fagundes, combining strategy and curiosity on how things work to develop editorial projects, visual identities and posters for cultural institutions as well as corporate clients.

Pedro Veneziano is a São Paulo-based graphic designer and art director who plays with multiple visual languages in his works, creating eye-catching imagery for brands, people, and cultural projects.

P092–093

Denis Yılmaz

denisyilmaz.de

Denis Yılmaz is a trained media designer for prints and previously studied graphic design in the University of the Arts Berlin in the class of Professor Fons Hickmann. Denis mainly focuses on working in typography, CGI, and editorial design. Furthermore, he is working as a freelance full-stack web developer and web designer.

P141

Diego Pinilla Amaya

behance.net/DiegoPinillaAmaya

Diego Pinilla Amaya is a Colombian art director and graphic designer who lives between Buenos Aires, Bogota, and New York. He is passionate about design. And the forms in his design are responsive to the social development. His works explore the boundaries of visual communication and contemporary issues through smart design.

P165

Dora Balla

balladora.hu

Dora Balla is a graphic designer, researcher, and writer. She graduated from the Moholy-Nagy University of Art and Design in 1998 and has worked there as a professor since 2007. Since 2015 she has been publishing several art books based on complex graphics and typographic projects. And as an exhibiting artist, she is an active member of the Hungarian and international graphics and art circles.

P168–169, P172–173

EBstudio (Elvis Benicio, Diego Bolgioni)

behance.net/elvisbenicio
behance.net/diegobolgioni

Elvis Benicio is a visual designer and art director with multi-disciplinary skills of cutting-edge aesthetics and craft. Diego Bolgioni is an art director and graphic designer based in São Paulo, Brazil, working with love on branding, editorial design, and digital design.

P012–013

eltipo

eltipographic.com

Born in the 80's, graphic artist eltipo is an all-around independent designer who specialises in both hand-drawn and computer vectorised typography, lettering, illustration, and graphic design. His murals can be seen in several hot retail and hospitality locations, and his works contributed to completing the look of award-winning interiors.

P218–219

Ermolaev Bureau

ermolaevbureau.com

Ermolaev Bureau is a graphic design studio specialised in visual brand creation, visual strategy development, and project implementation in the sphere of corporate and consumer's communication and aesthetics.

P088–089

Ewelina Gąska, Marta Frączek

ewelinagaska.com
behance.net/copyfm972d

Ewelina Gąska is an illustrator, graphic designer and graduate of the Polish Fine Arts Academy. In her work, she is not afraid of bold colours and the use of numerous patterns. Marta Frączek always tries to tell good stories. She likes to sew ideas, words, emotions, images, and sounds together to create an engaging communication.

P062–063

Fatih Hardal

behance.net/fatihhardal

Fatih Hardal is a designer from Turkey who currently lives and works in Istanbul. His biggest ambition is to make works socially useful.

P148–149, P163

Federico Leggio

federicoleggio.it

Federico Leggio is a graphic designer based in Sicily, Italy. He focuses on brand identity and visual design, but he likes to play with simple animations as well.

P130

Figure

figure-studio.com

Figure is a creative graphic design studio specialising in branding and visual identity. Figure designs striking images for fearless people and materialises coherent solutions from a process where nothing is left to chance.

P040, P052–053, P184–185

Forth + Back

forthandback.la

Forth + Back is a multidisciplinary design studio based in Los Angeles, California, founded by Nikolos Killian and Tanner Woodbury. They enjoy designing all kinds of works and stay curious to share their curiosities with others.

P186–187

Foxrabbit Studio

foxrabbit.pl

Foxrabbit is an independent Warsaw-based design studio delivering clear, elegant design solutions across multiple platforms. They specialise in graphic design, website, interface design, branding, and photography.

P076–077

FUNDAMENTAL

behance.net/Fundamental-studio

FUNDAMENTAL is a creative studio in Hong Kong, China. They believe that substantial communication is the key to creating and providing the best designs and solutions to their clients.

P176

Futura

byfutura.com/en/

Futura is a creative studio and wants to change the world. They wish they could find the cure for cancer but they will not. Instead, they create great brands, provocative images, beautiful objects, comfortable spaces, and user-friendly interfaces. That is their way to improve the quality of life of those they reach.

P022–023

Gao Yang

behance.net/wqxnc

Gao Yang is a Chinese designer who just wants to make beautiful things, even if nobody cares.

P102

Good Morning Design

gd-morning.org/jim

Co-founded by Jim Wong, Good Morning Design is an independent studio that specialises in visual identity, prints, and publications. Their works have been selected for numerous international design awards and published in international design magazines and publications.

P041

Guadalupe Peyrallo

behance.net/guadapeyrallo

Guadalupe Peyrallo is a graphic designer in Buenos Aires, focusing on branding and digital design.

P174

h3l™ Branding Agency

h3lweb.com

h3l™ Branding Agency is an independent and multicultural agency that stands out for its innovative ideas and conceptual work. The agency develops commercial and artistic projects of global incidence, published by many international publications.

P016–017

Hato

hato.co

Hato specialises in using design to engage and inspire communities and people. They work with some of the world's most innovative social networks, cultural institutions, lifestyle brands, and small-scale community groups. Their projects focus on giving people the tools to collaborate and express their ideas through design.

P126–129

Hunk Xing, KimYeonhee

behance.net/ihunk
kimyeonhee.com

Hunk Xing is a graphic designer whose recent works have been award the "Zcool Poster Design" and nominated as "Zcool Web Design." KimYeonhee is a design enthusiast based in Hangzhou, China.

P112–115

Jakub Malec "Serge"

behance.net/JakubMalec

Jakub Malec "Serge" is a freelance digital artist in Poland.

P104–105

Jérémie Solomon

jeremiesolomon.fr

Jérémie Solomon is an independent art director and printmaker based in Paris. He started studying drawing and traditional oil painting in Belgium. His latest research focuses on mixing graphic design and new technologies with traditional printmaking techniques.

P131, P132–133

Joan Ramon Pastor (Wete)

studiowete.com

Joan Ramon Pastor also known as Wete is a Spanish graphic designer based in Barcelona. Wete loves letterforms and typography and believes in the complexity of easy things. He actually runs his own studio Wete, a small and independent graphic design studio, specialising in art direction, typography, graphic design, and illustration.

P208–209, P210, P211, P212–213

JOEFANGSTUDIO

joefangstudio.com

Named after the director Joe Fang, JOEFANGSTUDIO takes part in music designs, event planning, brand planning, and art installation. The goal of the studio is to condense the creativity found in daily life to unique and fun designs.

P192–193

Johanna Dahmer, Lena Cramer

behance.net/johannadahmer
behance.net/lenacrmr

Johanna Dahmer and Lena Cramer studied Retail Design (BA) and Communication Design (MA) at the Peter Behrens School of Arts in Düsseldorf, Germany. They like to develop holistic concepts for events and especially for food themes, combining with typography, illustration, and photography.

P010–011

José Bernabé

josebernabe.com

José Bernabé is a designer and illustrator based in Amsterdam. He uses a mix of typeface, lettering, and illustration into digital and traditional techniques, achieving visual solutions with a vibrant colourful artwork, dedicated to the shapes, and flexible in styles depending on the communication to deliver.

P206–207

Kai Damian Matthiesen

kai-matthiesen.com

Kai Damian Matthiesen is a graphic designer holding a master's degree from the Royal College of Art in visual communication and a bachelor's degree from the London College of Communication in graphic design/typography. His works focus on bespoke creative solutions with an emphasis on clear and strong typographic designs.

P205

Karolína Pálková

behance.net/Karolina_Palkova

Karolína Pálková is a designer from Brno, Czech Republic.

P196–197

Kevin Lam

urfd.net

Kevin Lam is a graphic designer from Hong Kong, China and he is currently based in Brisbane. He graduated from Queensland College of Art in 2011 with a bachelor of design specialising in visual communication. His passion grew when he worked in a small studio and is ready to take on new challenges.

P200–201

Krisztian Tabori

ktabori.xyz

Krisztian Tabori is a creative professional from Budapest who currently resides in Copenhagen, Denmark. He has extended his knowledge in service design (UI/UX) and art direction. Also, he likes photography and travelling.

P122–123

Lucía Izco

luciaizco.myportfolio.com

Lucía Izco is a freelance 2D graphic designer in Buenos Aires, Argentina.

P134–135

Lully Duque, Laura Cárdenas

lullyduque.myportfolio.com
behance.net/lauracardenasa

Lully Duque and Laura Cárdenas are two Colombian graphic designers who work together on the development of personal projects. They both have a big interest in typography and graphic composition that has led them to create a wide range of visual projects.

P070–071

Mathieu Delestre

buroneko.com

Mathieu Delestre is a Paris-based multidisciplinary freelance designer specialising in print and digital graphic identity since 2005. He works mostly in the luxury and cultural sectors. The different facets of his works cover a wide spectrum of styles and graphics universes, allowing him to evolve in many areas such as graphic identity, illustration, layout, and collage.

P180–181

Max Genesiis

maxgenesiis.com

Max Genesiis is an art director and CD cover artist based in Minsk, Belarus. His specialisation is CD covers and promotional posters. He likes mixing dark colours with something bright in his design.

P164

Moby Digg

mobydigg.de

Moby Digg is a digital design studio, engaging in versatile conceptual and visual projects. Their tasks range from brand-strategy, branding visual identities, and web-development of complex appearances. Moby Digg focuses on combining the advantages of design and technology.

P156–157

Monumento

monumento.co

Monumento is a creative office based in Monterrey, Mexico, focusing on tailored concepts for premium brands. They specialise in branding, art direction, editorial and print design, websites and digital platforms, space creation, and creative strategy for clients that strive for modern culture.

P094–095

Muhammad Ridzwan Sakamat

behance.net/helloframeone

Muhammad Ridzwan Sakamat is the co-founder of Frame One. As an art director, digital and concept artist based in Malaysia, he makes 3D key visuals of digital art, typography, and motion graphic.

P216–217

Murmure

murmure.me

Based in Caen and Paris, Murmure is a French creative communications agency specialising in the strong visual identity. Led by two art directors Paul Ressencourt and Julien Alirol, the agency creates singular creative projects, aesthetic and adapts to its customers' problems.

P028–029

Nóra Kaszanyi

behance.net/norakaszanyi

Nóra Kaszanyi is a freelance graphic designer based in Budapest, Hungary.

P198

Olga Tkachenko

olgaplane.dribbble.com

Olga Tkachenko is a visual designer from Lviv, Ukraine.

P064–065

Paloma Pizarro

palomapizarro.com

Paloma Pizarro studied graphic design in Toulouse Lautrec Institute in Lima, Peru. He finished his studies in 2012. He has been working as a freelancer for the past three years on all kind of projects, from corporative branding to album covers and illustrations.

P177

Paperlux Studio

paperlux.com

Paperlux Studio was established in 2006 with a remarkably unconventional team assembled at the headquarters in Hamburg's dynamic Schanzenviertel District.

P175

Pengguin

pengguin.hk

Pengguin is a multidisciplinary design studio based in Hong Kong, China. Found by the design duo— Todd Lam and Soho So, who believe in good design should always give a positive energy and visual satisfaction. They are also a storyteller, keeping on sharing different stories and concepts by catching the chemistry between space and visual context.

P024–025

Pinchof

pinchof.sk

Pinchof is a visual collaborative incubator based in Bratislava and Lučenec, Slovak.

P026–027

Piotr Wątroba

krolowalama.pl

Piotr Wątroba is a multidisciplinary graphic designer from Poland.

P060–061

Pouya Ahmadi

pouyaahmadi.com

Pouya Ahmadi is a graphic designer, researcher, and educator. He is the editor of the journal *Amalgam*, assistant professor of graphic design at the University of Illinois at Chicago, and editorial board member of the magazine *Neshan*.

P144–145

Sagmeister & Walsh

sagmeisterwalsh.com

Sagmeister & Walsh is a creative agency based in New York City. They are a full-service studio providing strategy, design, and production across all platforms. They specialise in brand identities, campaigns, social strategy, content creation, commercials, websites, apps, books, environments, and more.

P048–049

Sergey Skip

sergeyskip.com

Sergey Skip is a Russian art director and designer living in Berlin.

P220–221, P222–223

Shanti Sparrow

shantisparrow.com

Shanti Sparrow is an award-winning Australian graphic designer, illustrator, lecturer, and dreamer. She has been freelancing internationally and working within boutique studios for the last decade. Sparrow is also named one of 33 Women Doing Amazing Things in Graphic Design along with design superstars Paula Sher, Jessica Walsh, and Debbie Millman.

P032–033, P098–099

Shui Lun Fan

fanshuilun.com

Shui Lun Fan graduated from the Hong Kong Polytechnic University and is now a communication designer based in Hong Kong, China.

P050–051

Sofía Mele

sofimele.com

Sofía Mele was born in 1993, Argentina. She studied graphic design at the University of Buenos Aires. She is also a muralist. Since 2011 she has been an assistant of the artist Adriana Carambia.

P178

Stepan Solodkov

behance.net/mrshadows

Stepan Solodkov is an individual designer based in Moscow, Russia. He has won the awards of Designer of the Year in ADC*Estonia 2018.

P054–057

Stephan Bovenschen

behance.net/StephanBovenschen

Stephan Bovenschen is a communication design student at the University of Applied Sciences in Augsburg, Germany. His main focus is on visual communication, typography, and graphic design. Together with other designers, he founded &Kollegen—a studio that tries to push forward special projects and ideas during spare time.

P150–151

Stockholm Design Lab (SDL)

stockholmdesignlab.se

SDL is one of Europe's most highly respected design companies. Founded by Björn Kusoffsky in 1998, SDL transforms brands and businesses with simple remarkable ideas.

P194–195

Studio Feixen

studiofeixen.ch

Studio Feixen is an independent design studio based in Lucerne, Switzerland that creates visual concepts. They focus specifically on nothing in particular. Whether it is graphic design, interior design, fashion design, type design, or animation—as long as it challenges them— they are interested.

P086–087

studio fnt
studiofnt.com

Studio fnt is a Seoul-based graphic design studio that works on prints, identities, interactive/digital media, and more. They collect fragmented and straying thoughts and then organise and transform those thoughts into relevant forms.

P146–147

This is Pacifica
thisispacifica.com

Pacifica is an independent communication studio based in Porto, Portugal, established in 2007 by Pedro Serrão, Pedro Mesquita, and Filipe Mesquita.

P142–143

Thomas Neulinger
thomasneulinger.com

Thomas Neulinger is a freelance art director and graphic designer based in Austria. In addition to his personal work, he creates conceptual art and design for prints, brands, websites, record covers, and publications.

P158–159

Tina Touli
tinatouli.com

Tina Touli is a London-based creative director, graphic communication designer, and educator. She currently runs her own multidisciplinary design studio—Tina Touli Design, and she teaches at Central Saint Martins, University of the Arts London. She worked for various clients including Adobe and UAL and had the honour to be selected by Magazine *Print* as one of the 15 best young designers in the world, aged under 30.

P058, P138–139, P140

Transwhite Studio
transwhite.cn

Transwhite Studio is a multifaceted studio featuring experimental design as well as a medium for communication with a primary focus on graphic design, expanding its role to include art exhibitions, social events, and other collaborations with different agencies in various fields.

P084–085

Tseng Kuo Chan
behance.net/tsengreen

Tseng Kuo Chan is a graphic designer based in Taipei, China. His works have been selected and published in *Design360°* and *Asian Pacific Design*. Currently, Tseng is working as a freelancer, specialising in graphic design, including CIS, VI, branding, book cover, magazine layout, art and cultural performance, exhibition's identity design.

P014–015, P059

Txaber Mentxaka
txaber.net

Born in 1969 in Bilbao, Spain, Txaber Mentxaka graduated in graphic design in 1992. After a career-spanning for more than twenty-five years in agencies, he invested in graphic experimentation which led him to develop his skills in 3D creation. His fascination with typography has allowed him to create a series of 3D typographic styles that can be seen in his works.

P228–229, P230–232

UVMW
uv-warsaw.com

UVMW is a team of designers, good at creating unusual branding and visual communication projects. Developing lots of creative solutions for cultural and business issues, they have done many untypical branding tasks, from small forms to big identity systems and multichannel advertising campaigns.

P100–101

Vicente García Morillo
vicentemorillo.com

Vicente García Morillo is a creative director, graphic designer, and illustrator whose works span across advertising, fashion, editorial, and digital design. His career in creativity started from a young age in his hometown in Spain. Vicente is the co-founder of the WeAre project, as well a creative director of New York multidisciplinary design studio—Burn & Broad.

P190–191

Voskhod Branding
voskhod.agency

Voskhod is the number-one independent creative agency in Russia. They are located in Yekaterinburg. Voskhod is advertising without any borders—geographical, national, or genre ones. Their works have received high marks of international festivals and this is evidenced by nine Cannes Lions and many other prestigious awards in the sphere of advertising.

P082–083

Woka Studio
wearewoka.com

Woka is a Spain-based studio helping brands and organisations to think big, resolve communication strategies without using typical things.

P030–031

Yaxu Han
yaxuhan.com

Yaxu Han is a 23-year-old designer, born and raised in Beijing, China. She fueled her passion for art at a young age. Yaxu loves creating an unconventional and whimsical design to inspire change.

P090–091

ACKNOWLEDGEMENTS

We would like to express our gratitude to all of the designers and companies
for their generous contribution of images, ideas, and concepts. We are also very
grateful to many other people whose names do not appear in the credits but who
made specific contributions and provided support. Without them, the successful
compilation of this book would not be possible. Special thanks to all of the
contributors for sharing their innovation and creativity with all of our readers
around the world.